OLD ENGLISH
FARMHOUSES

OLD ENGLISH FARMHOUSES

BILL LAWS

PHOTOGRAPHY BY

ANDREW BUTLER

COLLINS & BROWN

HALF-TITLE PAGE
FULMODESTONE
*A shepherd, his dog and two sheep
decorate the central pediment at The
Hall in Fulmodestone, Norfolk.*

First published in Great Britain in 1992
by Collins & Brown Limited
Mercury House
195 Knightsbridge
London SW7 1RE

British Library Cataloguing-in-Publication Data.
A catalogue record for this book
is available from the British Library.

ISBN 1 85585 089 3 (hardback edition)
ISBN 1 85585 119 9 (paperback edition)

Conceived, edited and designed by Collins & Brown

EDITORIAL DIRECTOR : Gabrielle Townsend
EDITOR : Jennifer Chilvers
ART DIRECTOR : Roger Bristow
DESIGNER : Gail Jones
MAPS : Andrew Farmer

Filmset by Servis Filmsetting Ltd, Manchester
Reproduction by J. Film, Singapore
Printed and bound in Hong Kong

TITLE PAGE
DUNTISBOURNE LEER
*Dovecots in the Cotswold stone walls
of a Gloucestershire farm cottage.*

CONTENTS

SCOTLAND

NORTHERN
ENGLAND

York

Manchester

WALES

Birmingham

Norwich

EASTERN
ENGLAND

MIDDLE ENGLAND

London

Canterbury

WESTERN
ENGLAND

SOUTHERN
ENGLAND

Exeter

FOREWORD

What are those blue remembered hills,
What spires, what farms are those?
A. E. HOUSMAN

THE TRADITIONAL FARMHOUSES of England are remarkably diverse. From Devon's cob and thatch to the flat blackstones of Cumbria, from the half-timbered and yellow-wash of the Weald to Norfolk's knapped flint and red brick, and from the hill-hugging crofts of the Welsh borders to the chilly limestone of the Cotswold manor, the range of vernacular styles is impressive.

Rooted in a past which reaches back into pre-Roman times and flowering in the sixteenth and seventeenth centuries when the vernacular tradition was at its peak, these buildings form the central architectural feature of the English countryside. Their designs colour our judgement about what is desirable and right for the landscape. Yet they face an uncertain future.

British agriculture is changing with devastating speed. In the time between the first flight of a manned aeroplane and the landing of men on the moon, the farming community has pared its workforce to the bone and turned itself from a co-operative way of life into a competitive industry. The English farmhouse has become a victim of change. Like hay ricks and hedges, woodlands and duck ponds, the working farmhouses of England have disappeared one by one. Some have been converted into non-farming, family homes, others have become mere mounds of rubble by the roadside. In years to come, as small, low-income farmers are squeezed out of business and large farms grow even larger, many more will be taken out of service.

Traditional farmhouses are among the most vulnerable buildings in Britain today. This book aims to explore their diverse styles, probe their historical background and celebrate their local importance before it is too late.

LEFT: BREWERSTREET FARM
The old English farmhouse holds a special place in the popular imagination and each has an architectural tale to tell. This Wealden house at Bletchingley in Surrey, with its roof of Horsham slate and its central hall flanked by a bay at either end, was built in the fifteenth century. Brewerstreet is a typical product of the wooded Weald of the south-east.

CHAPTER ONE

CROSSING THE THRESHOLD

The old barn embodied practices which had suffered no mutilation at the hands of time. Standing before this abraded pile ... the mind dwelt upon its past history, with a satisfied sense of functional continuity throughout—a feeling almost of gratitude, and quite of pride ...
THOMAS HARDY

FARMERS MAY NOT HOLD the title of being the oldest profession on earth, but they could justifiably lay claim to it. This land was shaped by farmers and their farmhouses have patterned the landscape for at least 5,000 years—the earliest permanent structure to be built on the British mainland was either a farm or a temple and, given the need for food and warmth before worship, the farm probably came first. Understandably, the farmhouse was built to last and, down the centuries, it has become the finest expression of the dynamics of vernacular building, in the best tradition of architecture without architects.

Some farming terms, like 'threshold', the place where corn was threshed, have crept into everyday usage and taken on a new meaning. Yet the word 'farmhouse', as a building distinct from the farm, was virtually unknown until the late sixteenth century. The word 'farm' was derived from the Latin, *firma*, signifying a fixed payment, rent or lease and referred to a parcel of land let, or 'farmed out', by a landowner. However, the first farms were established by neolithic tribes who eschewed nomadic hunting and gathering practices

ABOVE: STONE DRAGON
Rarely ostentatious and seldom heavily decorated, the farmhouse was designed to be as much a functional building as the barn or byre. Some, however, are richly adorned. This carved finial stands on the parapeted roof of Little Toller Farm in Dorset.

LEFT: MYERS GARTH FARM
Unmistakably northern, this farmhouse in the Yorkshire Dales near Aysgarth is walled and roofed in local stone. Built at least three hundred years ago by farmers who were happy to spend their money on buildings which honestly reflected local styles and traditions, the farmhouse was made to last.

ABOVE: VERNACULAR TRADITION
Farms were built of local materials, by local craftspeople to local designs and the flowering of farmhouse architecture in the sixteenth and seventeenth centuries came at a time when the vernacular tradition was at its peak. As farming practices change, farms and farm buildings face an uncertain future. This detail is from Cosby House barn in Leicestershire.

for a more settled slash, burn and grow economy. They grazed their sheep on the green hills of England long before the island became separated from the French coast and, with fire and stone, felled the forests and sowed their grains of emmer wheat on the burnt ground.

Their temporary huts of mud and turf gave way to more permanent timber-framed or stone-walled homes and spread in supportable colonies along the forest fringes and river banks. In lowland areas traces of this prehistory, the storage pits and hut circles, have disappeared. In the uplands, several sites have survived. On Devon's Dartmoor, the granite debris of a boundary wall still encircles the remains of a lonely farmstead at Grimspound. Within the circle stood the round stone huts, a mere six to twelve feet in diameter, where the herdspeople and their animals shared an intimate coexistence. Grimspound is a bleak moorland settlement in stark contrast to a later settlement at Chysauster in Cornwall where a group of farmhouses lined a curved street in neat, opposing pairs, like some carefully planned, suburban development.

Chysauster predates the Roman invasion and, in her 'Guide to the Prehistoric and Roman Monuments in England and Wales', Jacquetta Hawkes puts flesh on these bare bones of Iron Age life: '. . . the sun glaring in the courtyard where dogs lie on the paving, the rooms dark as caves, a woman sweating as she pounds away with the heavy grindstone, small children kept safely in sight by the closed door of the passageway. All a little smelly and untidy, but not too uncomfortable and wonderfully companionable.'

Like farmers down the ages, these people depended on a mixed economy and at Chysauster they traded in tin, shouldering their packs of ore and carrying them to St Michael's Mount from where the ore was shipped to France. The countryside through which they passed was well settled and their track, surfaced with brushwood bundles against the mud, meandered through a cultivated countryside and threaded its way along a necklace of pocket-sized hamlets built of stone or woven hazel poles daubed with clay.

When the first Roman ship ground its prow against the shingle of the southern shores, the landing legionaries found not a wild frontierland inhabited by roaming savages, but a tamed and pacified land farmed by people with a settled way of life and an established culture. Except in the west and north, that culture did not survive as the Romans superimposed their Mediterranean designs, materials and technology, together with their crops of wheat and barley, peas and beans. The Latin colonists also came to cultivate and the Roman villa was more of a working farm than a well-appointed, centrally-heated home. Small farms had a central hall flanked by wings to house slaves and servants, while the larger, manorial farms tucked the farm buildings away behind grand, porticoed frontages.

When the empire collapsed, the Romans were succeeded by barbarous tribes, snapping like wolves at the heels of the retreating armies. Within two centuries, the plundering wolves had turned into domesticated dogs and the piratical Saxon, Angle and Jute took to farming. The Saxons placed their organizational framework around the bare and run-down body of the British mainland, reducing the twelve English kingdoms to Wessex, East Anglia, Mercia and Northumbria, and dividing each into manageable manorial units

LEFT: HALL HOUSE
Many of the best examples of the English farmhouse still serve the farming community. Others, like this fifteenth-century Wealden hall house at the Weald and Downland Open Air Museum at Singleton in West Sussex, have been preserved by museums.

ABOVE: GRANITE
Stone cleared from the fields was used in boundary walls and buildings. The use of local materials means that the farms are in close harmony with the surrounding landscape.

with the peasant held in servitude. By the time Harold, the last Saxon king, lay dying on Hastings' battlefield, the British people were already worshipping in stone churches, farming fields corrugated into open ridge and furrow strips and living in compact villages whose names and boundaries had been fixed by the Saxons.

At this period the traceable past of the traditional farmhouse emerges. The Anglo-Saxons had built hall houses, which they preferred, and the Celtic-influenced longhouses, and had placed them on fresh sites away from the old Romano-British settlements where perhaps the scent of spilt blood was still strong. For the next 500 years, English farmers lived out their brief lives in huts of small timber, mud and straw, and homes of stone. Altered and adapted by subsequent generations of tenants and owners, these two characteristic buildings, the hall house and longhouse, rather than the circular Viking hut or ingenious Roman villa, became the prototype for English farmhouses. They did not remain in their original state for very long: 'Our farmers round, well pleased with constant gain,/ Like other farmers, flourish and complain,' wrote the eighteenth-century George Crabbe. The most common complaint levelled against those early farmhouses concerned their lack of space and privacy.

Imagine a Domesday settlement on the banks of the Thames, grouped around a stone-built manor house with adjoining stables. Outside its surrounding wooden palisade, the timber-framed forge, priest's house, mill and inn line the village road which wanders off, beyond the huts of serfs and villeins, past the great tithe barn, village bakehouse, Saxon or Norman church and graveyard into the outlying fields. The manor is a hall house, a barn-like, single-roomed hall where the family and their immediate servants live, sleeping on straw mattresses and eating at trestle tables. The smoky interior is warmed—heated would be too strong a word—by a central fire vented through an opening in the thatch above. Walls are hung with tapestries and hard floors are given a high shine by sprinkling ox blood on the earth and pounding the ground smooth.

The first departure from this communal way of life occurred when the master of the house, in need of a little draughtproof privacy, placed a screen across one end of the hall to form a separate chamber.

ABOVE: OPPORTUNISTS
The cost of transporting good building stone into an area was beyond the means of the average farmer who had to make do with whatever came to hand. Cut stone, flint and brick has been incorporated into this barn wall near Wool in Dorset.

The next development, which in agricultural terms was as revolutionary as the invention of the plough, was the introduction of the chimney in the thirteenth and fourteenth centuries. (The position of the hall and former hearth in an old farmhouse can often be established by the presence of smoke-blackened timbers in the loft above.) Constructed over the existing fire, the chimney divided up the hall. The lower chamber was partitioned off and a second chamber was built above.

Once the living quarters of master and servant had been screened off, the inclination to separate the social orders still further gathered momentum. The farmhouse grew with the addition of one or two side wings and the servants were banished to small rooms in the garret, over the buttery where the beer was brewed or above the pantry where dry stores were kept. The size of the wing, which on a timber-framed building could be jettied out to provide extra space, was an indication of the farmer's prosperity. Further indications were the disappearance of the old-fashioned, shuttered windows and

LEFT: DARTMOOR LONGHOUSE
One of the earliest farmhouse designs was the linear longhouse where the inner room, hall, cross-passage and shippon all lay under one roof. Sanders, a near-perfect, late medieval example at Lettaford in Devon, has been rescued for the nation by the Landmark Trust.

the appearance of small panels of glass, set in diamond-shaped leads to let the rainwater run from them. A staircase replaced the ladder, and upper floors were made of a smooth layer of gypsum spread on rushes or reeds laid across the joists. Bed chambers were given feather beds, walls were hung with painted cloths and expensive pewter took the place of wooden dishes and candlesticks. Manor farms like these were already flourishing in the vales and valleys of Kent in early Tudor times, although neighbouring farms lower down the social scale might still consist of only three rooms, the hall, kitchen and chamber.

The upland longhouse or laithe-house was distinctly different. Whereas on the hall-house plan animals were housed in a separate byre nearby, the longhouse farmer and his family shared the same sheltering roof with their stock. Thirty to forty feet long and fifteen to eighteen feet wide, with a cross-passage between the animals and their masters, the longhouse died out in the eastern lowlands 400 years ago. However, in the highland zone it was still being built in the

RIGHT: WEATHERBOARDING
The spiralling price of grain in the sixteenth and seventeenth centuries led to a corresponding increase in farmers' incomes. The old habit of storing produce in the farmhouse gave way to purpose-built farm structures like this Hampshire granary, used to store grain which had been threshed but not milled.

LEFT: GRANGE FARM
The interior of this restored sixteenth-century barn at Grange Farm, Basing in Hampshire, demonstrates the exceptional craftsmanship which went into its construction. Often, more money and time went into the construction of buildings like this than into the farmhouse itself.

1800s and in remote western areas was not superseded until the twentieth-century passion for hacienda-style brick or concrete bungalows spread like an outbreak of blight across those regions.

The first and most obvious development was to close off the cross-passage against the byre on the animals' side. This left the herdsman and his family cooped up in a one-roomed dwelling, lit by the flickering flames from the gable-end fireplace, and the daylight filtering in through the wooden bars of the small, unglazed windows. To make the best use of the limited space and create a little privacy, the longhouse inhabitants either utilized the roof space, cramming a loft room reached by a roof ladder under the eaves, or partitioned off the single downstairs room to form a parlour on the cross-passage side and a kitchen beside the hearth.

In the late sixteenth century, most farmhouses were, like the longhouse, still humble, single-width dwellings. But economic prosperity brought a corresponding rush to build better, bigger and more permanent houses. The Great Rebuilding, identified by the

BELOW: PITCHING HOLE
An astute use of stone characterizes the look of farmhouses in upland regions. The stonework around this first-floor door on a Cumbrian barn has mellowed with age. The doorway was used to take in hay for storage, pitched up from a wagon below.

BELOW: PINK LIMEWASH
Rough stonework on the farmhouse was regularly given a coat of limewash to protect it from the elements. The datestone over the threshold of this farm at Orton in Cumbria coincides with the time when the Great Rebuilding movement reached the Lake District.

ABOVE: BRICK QUOINS
The use of brick, confined at first to the east and south of the country, gradually spread across England during the Middle Ages. Handmade and fired on site, the look of the brick varied according to the local clay and the heat of the homemade kiln. Here brickwork has been used to form the quoins on a flint wall.

landscape historian Professor W. G. Hoskins, edged across the country starting in the south-east at the beginning of the expansive Elizabethan age and reaching the north-west at least a century later. 'England was filling up with people, recovering vigorously from the long decline of late medieval times,' wrote Professor Hoskins. 'Industries were growing and needed in ever-increasing quantities such country products as leather and wool. There was far more money about and, as they do today in similar circumstances, farmers set about improving their houses.'

The changes were fast, furious and radical, but with such a geographical time lag that, while the Great Rebuilding had spent itself in the south and south-east by about 1650, the rebuilding of highland areas like Cumbria ran from around 1650 to 1750 and beyond. During this transitional period, many lowland farmhouses doubled in depth. Cross wings, gable wings and wings to take a new staircase were added. The tenant farmer might renovate rather than rebuild and many a medieval timbered hall house lies waiting to be rediscovered beneath its Georgian brick façade or grey, cement render. However, in the more affluent lowland areas, smaller farms were sometimes let out and new buildings, from the modest two-up and two-down to a more spacious four-up and four-down, took their place. Their names, Brickhouse, Stonehouse, New Farm, Newhall, Newton, New Croft and New Buildings Farm, were inscribed in careful copperplate script on the land maps. Until the 1850s, when machine-made materials had begun to reach even the remotest country areas, most developments were designed to improve the farmer's working conditions: a separate barn or byre for the longhouse, relieving the old byre for domestic use; a dairy, usually attached to the north side of the house and sunk in earth to improve coolness; a cat-slide roof run out over a cheese chamber or meat safe, a brewing cellar or a farm office.

The majority of the farmhouses described here were built during the sixteenth, seventeenth and eighteenth centuries, and although they emerged from the same rootstock, they did not conform to the same design. An amateur historian, armed with the right books, can classify a village church with enviable accuracy; the farmhouse,

ABOVE: FLINT AND BRICK
Lacing courses of bricks serve to reinforce a barn wall of flint and rough stone at Eastbury in Berkshire. Those bricks exposed to the greatest heat during firing have vitrified and turned a dark, grey-blue colour.

ABOVE: CIRCULAR STACK
The development of the chimney to replace the draughty opening in the roof was as revolutionary as the invention of the plough. Before brick became common in the upland areas, local stone had to be used for the chimney and flue. The circular stacks of Cumbria and the west country side-stepped the problem of shaping corner stones from rough rock.

although it might share the same antiquity, is too much the individual to fall into such precise categories since affluence, poverty and vernacular tradition conspired against uniformity.

As regional styles evolved and improved during the Great Rebuilding, the vernacular tradition approached its zenith. Although each farmer shared the same basic need for buildings which protected his family, his crops and his beasts, regional influences complicated the process of providing them. One district with a rich soil thrived while another less well endowed declined; one economy, like the Cotswold sheep industry, was continually expanding to meet demand while another, like the self-sufficient, upland farmer, subsisted on the margin between survival and starvation. Some people possessed a plentiful supply of natural building materials and could respond to the ebb and flow of international influence; others could barely find the means to replace the straw thatch on their humble two-roomed home. Thus the Cotswolds became noted for its multi-gabled, manor-like farmhouses while the West Midlands developed the crooked, black and white, half-timbered buildings; the Weald of Kent produced close-timbered and colour-washed buildings, while Fenland farmers built brick and flint farmhouses with vaulting Dutch gables.

Within the regions, local variations evolved so that, like the ears of wheat in a field of corn, no two farmhouses were exactly alike. Function and local fashion governed form and the look of the farmhouse was sometimes common only to a particular area, sometimes only to a particular parish.

England before the Industrial Revolution was still a nation of country people with the rural community firmly focused upon itself. As the wheels of commerce turned, each hub revolved around the country parish in an evolutionary process begun 3,000 years before the birth of Christ. The labourer sowed, hoed and cut the corn while the miller ground the grain. The farmer raised his flesh and fowl while the butcher killed and sold it. The wheelwright and blacksmith serviced the carter who ferried the village produce to market and fetched new building stone from the parish quarry and timber from the nearby wood. Local craftspeople relied on these materials to

ABOVE: MAKING ECONOMIES
Cheap building materials like Welsh slate and machine-made bricks eventually brought the vernacular tradition to an end. Here, in the exposed south-west, Cornish slate has been hung on roof, walls and chimney to protect them from the elements.

construct buildings whose designs were already well tried and tested. The farmer himself looked to the village craftspeople to erect his home and make his furniture.

Not that the architect was entirely absent from the scene. While farmhouse design was generally confined to practical considerations, the farmer and landowner built according to their means and there were those, especially in the south and east, who could afford to take account of popular fashion. As early as 1747, a book of farmhouse patterns by Daniel Garrett became a best-seller; a similar book by Robert Beatson recommended the siting of the farmhouse away from the smells of the midden heap and the danger of fire from hay and corn stacks.

Today the traditional farmhouse and its furniture has itself acquired a fashionable appeal and a country-style kitchen, equipped with Sussex iron fireplate, ingle-nook fireplace, Welsh dresser, settle, rag rug, gate-legged table, ladder-backed chairs and wickerwork baskets, is considered appropriate in the most urban setting. It is a far

BELOW: DERBYSHIRE
These two views of farm barns emphasize the same use of different stone and the resulting local look of a place. The more pliable stone on this Derbyshire barn allowed the mason to build in regular, horizontal courses and create a neat finish at the gables. The projecting stones on both barns run right through the walls and help to bond the stonework.

BELOW: CUMBRIA
By contrast, the rough, rubble courses on this barn at Kentmere give it a rugged appearance. The stepped gable overcomes the difficulty of making a weatherproof seal between walls and roof. Typically, the bright coat of whitewash has been used on the farmhouse and not the barn.

cry from Mr William Bingley's experience in 1798 when he took lunch in a Welsh farmhouse, accompanied by the farmer and his family and 'a large, overgrown old sow devouring her dinner with considerable dissatisfaction on account of the short allowance, from a pail placed for her by the daughter in one corner of the room'.

Neither was sixteenth-century Bishop Joseph Hall enamoured by the internal arrangements of a farmhouse kitchen:

> ... whose thatched spars are furred with sluttish soote
> A whole inch thick, shining like blackmoor's brows,
> Through the smoke that downe the headlesse barrel blows.
> At his bed's feete feeden his stalled teame,
> The swine beneath, his pullen o'er the beame.

The bishop implied that living in such close proximity to the animals was a slovenly habit. There is no reason to suppose this farming family was any less houseproud than his own housekeeper.

RIGHT: BUILDER ARCHITECT
Most of the farmhouses illustrated here were built by the householder and his neighbours in the time-honoured tradition of architecture without architects, although specialists like the stonemason might have supervised the construction of items like this flint wall in Devon.

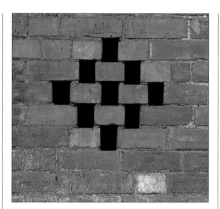

ABOVE: VENTILATION
The task of looking after our old farmhouses and farm buildings depends on the resources of farmers. Redundant details like the air holes in this brick barn near Abthorpe in Northamptonshire are sometimes lost during unsympathetic modernizations which, in their worst form, are acts of architectural vandalism.

Until a modicum of law and order was established in England, the farmer did well to construct his farmhouse with an eye on defence and, if necessary, share his hearth with his precious beasts. In northern England, the protective bastle farmhouse, in which the family lived directly above the byre, is still to be found, although no longer inhabited. In the case of the longhouse, the practice of keeping the cattle within shouting distance at the far end of the farmhouse still continued in remote western areas until well into the twentieth century.

Organizations like the National Trust and the Landmark Trust have successfully restored and preserved many farmhouses like these, while open-air museums like the West Midlands' Avoncroft Museum of Buildings and the Weald and Downland Open Air Museum in West Sussex have removed threatened farms to a place of safety and given them a new, if slightly unreal, lease of life in their grounds. An increasing number of privately owned farmhouses have been subjected to a second renovation which has sensitively exposed their original Elizabethan or Tudor past.

Yet for every farmhouse which has been restored or taken into care, there are a score more still functioning as working farms down some quiet country lane. Why then should we strive to preserve them when our stock of crumbling cathedrals and collapsing stately homes already strains the limited resources available to maintain the structural past? Although our understanding of heritage, the conservable past, has changed in the last thirty years, the significance of the humble homes of England has been slow to take root. These buildings, and farmhouses in particular, may not have the grand impact of a fifty-roomed Georgian mansion, but they are a crucial piece of the historical jigsaw. With their individual characters and their weathered good looks, farmhouses are an expression of regional identity. They are an echo of times past and a lesson in economy for the future. If they are to grace the countryside of our children's children, we need to appreciate them now.

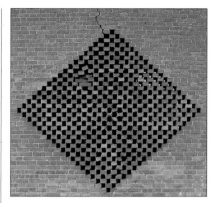

ABOVE: CRAFT AS ART
The contribution which traditional farms make to the rural scene may not be fully appreciated until they have been pulled down and replaced with buildings whose dull designs are common from Cornwall to Cumbria. Local details mean local distinctiveness.

CHAPTER TWO

SOUTHERN ENGLAND

The hills, the woods, the meadows, are all beautiful. Nothing wild
and bold, to be sure, but exceedingly pretty.
WILLIAM COBBETT

KENT, SURREY AND BERKSHIRE, the three counties which sit on
London's doorstep, have traditionally grown food for the
capital and drawn on its labour force to harvest Kent
cherries, Surrey strawberries and Berkshire pears. Sussex, Hampshire and, to a lesser extent, Wiltshire were also mindful of the
lucrative London market and expected to profit from it. Despite
having been intensively farmed for centuries, the countryside south
of the capital was known as the Garden of England: to the city fruit-
pickers, leaving the mean streets for the rolling Downs and rippling
cornfields, the Garden lived up to its name.

Today these counties look less like a garden and more like some
great estate which is being farmed with formidable efficiency. The old
oast houses are framed, not by hop gardens, but by a yellow sea of
oilseed rape and the tithe barns that once stored the medieval corn
harvest now house a mountain of potatoes and a fleet of tractors. The
landscape too has changed. The tidily wooded Weald; the green-
wood of the New Forest; Hampshire and Surrey's sandy heaths; the
Marlborough Downs, Berkshire Downs and Hampshire Downs and
the verdant dairy valleys of Thomas Hardy's Wessex are all subject to
the increasing pressures of a burgeoning population which needs new
homes, roads and factories.

In the south, the sixteenth-century Great Rebuilding had been
preceded by economic prosperity; like the Cotswolds and East
Anglia, areas like Hampshire and Sussex drew their early wealth from

LEFT: ARABLE ACRES
Stretching from the hop gardens of
Kent to Hampshire's New Forest,
the southern farmland enjoyed a
kind climate and a ready market for
produce. The farmers' fortunes,
founded on a predominantly 'horn
and corn' economy, resulted in a rich
variety of farmhouses. The Kennels,
set in parkland near Stourton in
Wiltshire, carries all the hallmarks
of a traditional rural building.

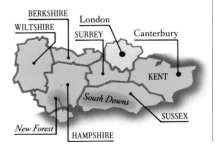

the sheep economy while the Weald, which in the fifteenth and sixteenth centuries was like one vast iron-smelting works, derived its profits from the iron ore of the Wealden sandstones. But the rebuilding, which transformed the face of domestic buildings in the sixteenth and seventeenth centuries, palls into insignificance when compared to the pre- and post-war building boom of the twentieth century. The urban influence is still spreading into the heartland of these southern counties.

The affluent air of those farmhouses which lie close to London is nothing new. Down the centuries, they were regularly given a fresh façade in accordance with the fashion of the day. A socially ambitious Berkshire farmer in the late Tudor period might conceal his timber-framed hall behind a brick frontage, only to have his grandson's grandson hide the elegant brickwork with a stucco finish, applying successively smooth coats of sand and lime, bound together with horsehair, across the brickwork.

In one sense, it was an unfortunate habit since many a classic farmhouse went unrecognized when historic or architecturally important buildings were listed and graded in the mid-twentieth century. Neither did the taste for a fashionable farmhouse meet with everyone's approval. When that irascible, nineteenth-century commentator William Cobbett found himself standing before one such farmhouse in Surrey, he railed against it. 'One end of this once plain and substantial house has been moulded into a parlour; and there was the mahogany table, and the fine chairs, and the fine glass, and all as bare-faced upstart as any stock-jobber in the kingdom can boast of.'

To Cobbett this farmhouse epitomized the growing gulf between landowner and landworker, proof-positive of the damaging effects of the Enclosure Movement. New agricultural ideas on crop rotation and the over-wintering of farm stock had led to a demand for hedged fields and controlled pastures and the enclosing of traditional open fields spread through the country from around 1750 to 1850. Too often enclosures were used to appropriate common land where villagers and small farmers gathered their winter fuel, snared wild rabbit or pastured their house cow. The neat new scenery of fenced-

ABOVE: TIMBER TRADITION
The early breakdown of the manorial system and the consequent rise of the yeoman farmer led to a demand for substantial, independent farmhouses. With good supplies of Wealden oak, the timber-frame tradition, seen here in a detail from Sheiling Farm (opposite), was assured.

RIGHT: WEALDEN HOUSE
The Wealden or yeoman's house, built throughout Sussex, Surrey and Kent, was a direct descendant of the medieval hall house. The two-storey windows at Sheiling Farm in Langley, Kent, indicate the position of the original hall.

ABOVE: FARM BELL
The vernacular architecture of any region mirrors the quality of the underlying rock and available timber. The geological formations in the south produced good clay for making the bricks which went into this building. The farm bell, wrung loud, would summon the farmer back from his fields.

RIGHT: WESTHANGER FARM
*On most Wealden farmhouses the
central hall, flanked by bays at either
end containing parlour, pantry,
buttery and bedchambers, sheltered
beneath a continuous roof. Some
farmhouses, like Westhanger, have
only a single bay.*

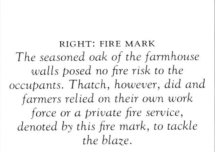

RIGHT: FIRE MARK
*The seasoned oak of the farmhouse
walls posed no fire risk to the
occupants. Thatch, however, did and
farmers relied on their own work
force or a private fire service,
denoted by this fire mark, to tackle
the blaze.*

off rectangular fields, insisted William Cobbett, was turning tenant farmers into landless labourers and causing the destruction of three out of every four farmhouses in the countryside around Windsor.

During rural rioting in the late summer of 1830, two-thirds of the incidents took place in the rich and fertile south and east as out-of-work labourers took their revenge on new farm machinery, the symbol, but not the cause, of their unemployment. Some farmers parked their machines in the farmyard and provided the saboteurs with hammers and free beer for the event, preferring the destruction of the threshing machine to the torching of their houses. Cobbett, who described the rioters as people in want with 'nothing to lose except their lives', had first-hand experience of their plight. Born in 1763 at Farnham, he had, at the age of eight, started work in a Surrey hop garden and could sympathize with the plight of enclosure victims like the labourers he met one morning repairing a road at Wrecklesham, Surrey.

Amongst them was an old playmate of mine. The account they gave of their situation was very dismal. The harvest was over early. The hop picking is now over; and now they are employed by the parish.

By the middle of the nineteenth century, the labourers' houses were 'beggarly in the extreme' while the profits from the newly enclosed land were making an ostentatious show in the façades of fashionable farmhouses. None were finer than those which stood in the Garden of England, set as they were within carting distance of one of the best markets for fresh farm produce in Europe.

The breakdown in the once dependable relationship between farmer and farmhand began at least 500 years earlier and can be traced in the development of the Wealden house, the most famous farmhouse of all. The Wealden house was also known as the yeoman's house, for in fifteenth-century Kent there was a strong tradition of independent freeholders. The local custom of partible inheritance, where property was divided among all the children, led to a proliferation of small farms and farmhouses, many of them based on the design of the Wealden house.

In its infancy the Wealden house was a stereotype of the Saxon hall, built of timber and wattle and daub, with its rectangular, single-storey hall open to the draughty rafters. Smoke from the fire on the floor drifted out through an opening in the thatch and the yeoman farmer slept and ate in the convivial if crowded company of his family, his workers and his dogs. Here casual exchanges about the state of the crops or the next day's labour would take place together with more formal meetings to discuss parochial affairs. While farming remained a largely co-operative exercise in basic survival, the Wealden hall served as the centrepiece of rural life.

Elements of this communal lifestyle persisted until well within living memory in northern and western regions where farm labourers continued to be billeted with the farming family. It did not last long in the south. In the absence of a dictatorial manorial system, the foundrymen farmers of Kent worked their fields when the iron-smelting industry moved north into the Midlands. In an agricultur-

ABOVE: KENTISH LANDMARK
The flyboard set into the side of the white, timber cowl acted like a weathervane and turned the cowl against the wind. Pans of sulphur were added to the coal or charcoal fires below to add colour and flavour to the drying hops.

RIGHT: GARDEN OF ENGLAND
Hops were first grown as a commercial crop in Kent in the sixteenth century, the flowers being used to clarify, preserve and flavour beer. In the mid-eighteenth century, nearly half the nation's hops were grown by Kent farmers.

ABOVE: OAST HOUSES
The southern counties grew food for the London market and drew on its labour-force during the picking season. The harvested hops were dried in the ivy-covered kilns, or oast houses, before being spread on the upper floor of the adjoining cooling house to be bagged for market.

28

The generous, close-spaced timbers of the farmhouse indicate no shortage of building oak in the neighbourhood. However, as woods were felled and replaced with fields, stocks of timber fell and prices rose. On later buildings, the timbers were set further apart.

ally expanding area like the Weald, the farmer was continually having to provide additional storage space for his crops or extra working rooms for processes like cheesemaking and during the Great Rebuilding the single hall was extended by adding two-storeyed cross wings at either end, the upper floor jettied out over the lower. In the timber-framed farms of northern and eastern England, where space was short, extra wings were built to give the farmhouse an H or U shape, but on the Wealden farmhouse, local tradition dictated that the wings remained under one continuous roof and did not project beyond the wall line. A chimney was inserted, generally in the centre of the house, and the familiar process of dividing and sub-dividing the open-plan hall into rooms or chambers took place. Gradually the labourers and their families were moved to their own quarters in

ABOVE: CRAFTED WOODWORK
A carved corbel supports an oriel window on Old Harrow Farm, near Egerton, Kent (opposite). The yeoman farmer expected, and could afford to pay for, a high standard of craftsmanship.

LEFT: OLD HARROW FARM
Regular applications of butter-yellow limewash not only helped to fill cracks in the wattle and daub, but also added a subtle dash of colour to the building shown opposite.

another part of the house, then to farm buildings shared with the animals and eventually into separate buildings altogether. 'Now each rich man has a rule to eat in secret,/ In a private parlour,' grumbled William Langland in the great fourteenth-century epic poem *Piers Plowman*.

The Wealden farmhouses, concentrated along the south-west slopes of the North Downs, had their generously proportioned timbers set close together, for the Weald was still rich in oak wood despite predictions that the iron masters and the later naval ship-builders would exhaust the native woods. And the yeoman worked with what the Weald had to offer—a landscape of small fields and woodland pockets, which dictated an intensive, vegetable-garden approach to farming. Fruit orchards, sheep, hops, pigeon and hogs fattened on the plentiful supplies of oak and beech nuts, all thrived. Each product, from the pigeon loft to the fruit store, required its own type of building, but none were more distinctive than the hop-drying oast house, built beside the farmhouse in the local vernacular style.

RIGHT: OLDE HOUSE
When this Wealden house at Harrietsham in Kent was built in the late fifteenth century, the central, open hall was beginning to lose favour in the south. Olde House may originally had have a two-storey window to light the hall.

RIGHT: CHANGING LANDSCAPES
The piecemeal enclosure of open ground had been taking place from the fourteenth century, but the pace of Parliamentary Enclosures speeded up the process during the seventeenth and eighteenth centuries. Common land was curtained off by neat, rectangular fields like these on Great Bookham Common in Surrey. Since then, many of the smaller fields and their hedgerows have been taken out.

LEFT: CROSSWAYS FARM
A patina of moss and lichens colours the roof of stone slates. The size of Crossways Farm, and the rich mix of materials which went into its construction, emphasizes the agricultural prosperity of the south.

BELOW: BRICKWORK
The use of brick in southern England was confined at first to religious buildings and large houses. Bricks like these on Crossways Farm near Abinger in Surrey (opposite) were moulded or rubbed to create decorative patterns. The S-shaped tie plates held a wrought-iron bar which ran through the building to prevent the walls from bellying out.

Hops had been growing wild in southern England long before they were introduced as a beer-preserving crop in the sixteenth century. When it became a cultivated cash crop, hop growing was centred on the Kent and Sussex Weald, parts of Surrey, Hampshire and, up in the West Midlands, in Hereford and Worcester. Grown and harvested in a hop garden (called a hop yard in the West Midlands), the hops had to be dried on the upper floor of an oast house (known as a hop kiln in the west) before being decanted into pockets or hop sacks. The early oast houses, two-storeyed, rectangular buildings, were replaced by the more familiar tower-shaped oast house, topped with a revolving cowl and built alongside a storage or cooling shed, in the early nineteenth century. Like so many of these southern farm buildings, the old oast house was eventually rendered redundant by modern methods.

Hops would not grow on the neighbouring downland which in the fifteenth and sixteenth centuries consisted of bare and treeless tracts of land, cleared of their native wildwood 6,000 years before by

BELOW: GALLETING
Small chips of stone or gallets were worked into the mortar joints at Crossways Farm (opposite) for ornamental puposes. In the Middle Ages however, galleting served the practical purpose of strengthening wide mortar joints.

neolithic farmers and subsequently kept under close control by grazing sheep. The North and South Downs and the downland of Wiltshire, Berkshire and Hampshire were all formed from the same thick layer of chalk which yielded little useful building stone, apart from flint and clunch, a rock-hard form of chalk. Where the chalk shelved down into the lowland valleys gouged out by the ice sheets of the last glaciation, the thin strata of sandstone, limestone and clays each contributed to the look of the local buildings.

A confusion of local names described these vernacular materials. There was malm stone, a hard limestone used in the walls of some of the South Downs villages, and Kentish rag, a rough and brittle rock, used by the Romans to build London's walls and by the farmers of Kent and its neighbouring counties to build farmhouses. Clunch by comparison was more flexible. A hard chalk cut into white building blocks, clunch appeared throughout Berkshire, Hampshire and Wiltshire, especially around Salisbury. It was too soft to form into door and window surrounds so the farmer would have to call out the

RIGHT: EARLY DIVERSIFICATION
A wide range of goods, from fruit and corn to wool and beef was produced on southern farms. It had to be stored or stabled in a complexity of different barns, byres and sheds like this multi-purpose barn near Wisborough in West Sussex.

RIGHT: LOCALLY MADE
With little standardization in the manufacture of locally made materials such as bricks and tiles, country buildings like this one near Bignor in Sussex made a minimal impact on its rural surroundings.

ABOVE: RAINPROOF
Wide eaves on the steep thatch helped to keep rainwater off the face of the farmhouse. However, a prevailing wind regularly blew the water back against the walls. Jettying out the first floor protected the lower half of the building from the worst of the weather.

LEFT: YEOMAN'S COTTAGE
This building at Bignor in Sussex illustrates how vernacular architecture followed no fixed rules. From its chimney of brick to its plinth of raw stone, this former shop makes a distinctive architectural contribution to the village.

bricklayer to build his door and window jambs. To the west, Grey Wethers or sarsens outcropped near the Marlborough Downs. Blocks of sarsens, some weighing up to fifty tons each, encircled the mystical Welsh Blue Stones at Stonehenge, but where they were used on the Wiltshire farmhouses, they were too tough to be more than roughly coursed into the walls.

Occasionally, and where the building stones permitted, the walls of the southern farmhouse were given a curious chequerboard look. Where Wiltshire and Hampshire bordered on Dorset, light lime-stone or greensand blocks were interspersed with black, knapped flint or dark bricks; in coastal Sussex a similar effect was created by mixing dark brick with light-coloured flint taken from the sea-shore. Another localized material was Bath stone, so highly prized that it was already being carted into other areas before the Norman

LEFT: FLINT INFILL
In the half-timbered farmhouse (opposite), the gaps between the timbers, rather than the frame itself, needed regular maintenance. One solution was to replace the conventional wattle and daub with brick. Here, unusually, knapped flints have been used.

RIGHT: STRAWBERRY HOLE
Like a scene from the pre-Enclosure days, this curiously named farmhouse stands out in the landscape near Northiam in East Sussex.

RIGHT: MONEY FROM MEAT
The symbol of a chained bull meant more to the farmer than a mere family crest. Agricultural innovations spread like wildfire through the south during the eighteenth century and resulted in improvements in stock management, crop husbandry and the livelihood of the farmers.

conquest. Only later did builders discover that the honey-gold stone was sensitive to pollution and tended to blacken in the city air; used on the Wiltshire farmhouses, especially those around Corsham where it could be cheaply taken from the local quarries, it kept its good looks in the clean, country air.

Bath stone was one of many different types of limestone found in the 300 mile long limestone belt which crosses the country from Dorset to Humberside. Sometimes of such poor quality that it was formed into farmhouse walls and hurriedly given a coat of plaster or render to conceal its imperfections, the limestone also yielded the mellow stone of the Cotswolds and north Wiltshire. The Wiltshire farmlands had prospered with their sheep, corn and riverside dairy pastures and the demure limestone farm buildings blended into the scenery like corncrakes in a cornfield. The farmhouses themselves were more modest versions of the high Gothic of the north Cotswolds with timber replacing iron window casements and stone lintels, and simple dormers in place of the grand Cotswold gable.

BELOW: BOATHOUSE FARM
Tile-hanging first appeared in southern England in the late seventeenth century, the tiles being hung on wooden battens fixed to the walls. Clay for the tiles was often dug and fired on the farmhouse site.

RIGHT: BROCKWELLS FARM
Terracotta tiles for wall hanging were sometimes cut into ornamental shapes finishing in a fish-tail or half-circle. On this farm at Isfield in Sussex the same tiles would have been used for roof and walls.

BELOW: CLAY COLOURS
Variations in the orange tones of the tiles came from both the quality of the clay used and the traditional method of wood-firing them.

ABOVE: PLASTER CLADDING
Bare plaster, finished with a bright coat of whitewash was like a canvass without a painting. Here at Oxenbridge (opposite), the plain plaster has been decorated with animal heads.

However, Cotswold slate, stone to the layman, was common to both the north Wiltshire and Gloucestershire farmhouse. Arguably the most attractive roof in all England, Cotswold slate, carpeted with lichens, was run out over farmhouse, cowshed and pigsty alike.

With Cotswold slate and Horsham stone, Cornish slate and small clay tiles, shingles and straw or reed thatch, the roofs of these southern farmhouses exhibited as great a variety of materials as did the wall stones. Thatch was thought to have been virtually universal on the smallholdings and farm cottages of the sixteenth and seventeenth centuries until excavations on an abandoned village on the North Downs revealed several farmsteads roofed in Cornish slate which would have been brought in by sea. By the late eighteenth century, huge quantities of Welsh slate were being shipped up the Thames and many a Kentish or Berkshire farmer was doubtless tempted to adopt this long-lasting and fireproof material when his old farm required reroofing. Despite having to rethatch every thirty years or so, many resisted the temptation.

Where wheat or rye was grown, and the straw harvested without being unkindly bruised, it was regularly recycled on the farmhouse roof. Even today, the concentration of thatched farms in the countryside around West Sussex, Hampshire and on into the western counties of Dorset and Devon is matched and overtaken only by the eastern counties of Norfolk and Suffolk. On the farms of the coastal plain south of Chichester and among the tea-cosy cottages of the New Forest, the straw thatch rolled across roof and gable, eye-shadowed diminutive dormer windows and swept down over the honeysuckled trellis-work of the porch. In appearance, it suited almost any building from the cob or brick and flint of Hampshire to the brick or sarsen stones of Wiltshire; in construction, it was so light that thin battens nailed across the oak rafters provided adequate support. Roofs of Cotswold or Horsham slate, which weighed up to one ton for every hundred square feet of cover, required far more substantial, and thus far more expensive, under-timbers.

Clay tiles were an acceptable substitute. In Marlborough, where a series of disastrous thatch fires in the seventeenth century led to an act of Parliament forbidding the use of thatch in the town for ever,

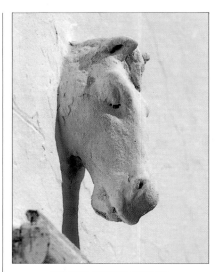

ABOVE: HORSE POWER
The horse replaced the oxe as a draught animal in the early eighteenth century and for the next two hundred years, until the advent of the tractor, the plough horse worked the land. In 1918 there were more than a million horses on British farms.

RIGHT: Oxenbridge
More common in eastern England, the practice of plastering timber-framed houses like this fifteenth-century Wealden hall house at Iden in Sussex was occasionally used to conceal inferior timberwork. A coat of plaster also gave the building a fresh and fashionable face-lift.

LEFT: GRANGE FARM
The plain face of Grange Farm at Basing in Hampshire demonstrates an early, and unpretentious, use of brick at the vernacular level. To avoid the ill-conceived, seventeenth-century window tax, several windows have been blocked off.

LEFT: HUMBLE SHEDS
The constructional detail that went into even the most modest farm building ensured that it would last for years. Some, like this open-fronted cattle shed, have outlived their original purpose.

LEFT: BUTLERS COMBE FARM
A group of brick-built and slate-roofed buildings cluster together to form a small hamlet on the edge of the chalk downlands. William Cobbett liked the neighbouring market town of Warminster: 'Everything belonging to it is good and solid'.

ABOVE: NEW TILES
A replacement roof of clay tiles laps the old stone slabs. Beneath, regular courses of knapped flint are interleaved between blocks of hand-cut stone.

the small clays replaced the straw. From as early as the thirteenth century, 'baked tiles' as they were sometimes called spread through the southern farmland. They were highly versatile. A roof of baked tile needed neither the relatively flat pitch of stone, required to prevent the heavy slabs sliding from the roof and maiming some unfortunate passer-by, nor the sharp pitch of thatch, set steep to throw off the rainwater before it could seep through the straw or reed. The shape of the southern farmhouse roofs changed gradually from the hipped roof of the Wealden house and the half-hipped Sussex farm to intricate constructions with cat-slides running from the ridge almost to the ground and wings jettied out from the front of the building in Berkshire and Hampshire. In Wiltshire, the hipped roof was relatively rare and the plain gabled roof more common. Porches and outhouses, incorporated into the main farmhouse as the need for extra rooms arose, added irregularities to the farmhouse. The plain clay tiles suited them all, carried as they were on undulating battens which gave the farmer's roof the seductive look of a rose-coloured bedspread.

The south-east was the first area to develop weather-tiling where clay tiles were hung on the vertical face of the half-timbered farmhouse. Sometimes confined to the upper floor or simply the exposed gables of the buildings as in the village of Bletchingley, Surrey, the practice spread through Kent, Surrey and Sussex and into Hampshire, Berkshire and Wiltshire during the eighteenth century. On early buildings the roof tile was used, but on later buildings tiles were cut into fanciful fish-tail or half-circle shapes for a more elaborate finish. Before the Industrial Revolution, plain tiles, like bricks, were made from the local clays, dug, moulded and fired on the farm where they were to be used. Official attempts to standardize the size of the tile as early as 1477 were ignored by the local tilemaker and regional sizes persisted—the Kent tile, for example, was marginally narrower than the Sussex tile.

In Kent, East Sussex and parts of Surrey, some of the brickwork subsequently disappeared behind weatherboarding when foreign softwoods were imported during the eighteenth century. Stained with tar on farm buildings, the weatherboarding of farmhouses was

ABOVE: ORNAMENTAL LEADWORK
Before the Industrial Revolution, lead was one of the few metals used on the English farmhouse. The material for this early seventeenth-century, dated downpipe may have come from the nearby Mendip Hills.

painted bright white with door and window frames picked out in black. Boarding was also used to clad timber-framed houses, although another material, the brick-tile, was becoming increasingly popular in the coastal areas of Kent and Sussex. The tile, sometimes called a mathematical tile or wall tile, with one face carefully moulded to resemble a brick, was developed in the New Forest. Nailed to horizontal battens on timber framework or set in plaster, the brick-tiles were pointed with mortar to look like real brickwork. Despite being exempt from the eighteenth-century brick taxes, brick-tiles were an expensive alternative to weatherboarding, but were readily adopted by the fashion-conscious farmer who wanted to give his house a face-lift.

The rising popularity of the brick-tile symbolizes the difference between southern and eastern areas and the distant north and west: in spite of its cost and inherent artificiality, it gave the old farmhouse the look of a new-born building and imparted an impression of affluence. Mr Cobbett would have disapproved.

RIGHT: MANOR FARM
The seventeenth-century Manor Farm with its ashlar walls and roof of weather-darkened tiles took advantage of the quality and quantity of good, local building stone around Stockton in Wiltshire.

RIGHT: WORKING LANDSCAPE
Morning mists rise on Wiltshire's wooded Vale of Pewsey.

CHAPTER THREE

WESTERN ENGLAND

. . . old builders, who worked when art was a living thing, had no respect for the work of the builders who went before them, but pulled down and altered as they thought fit; and why shouldn't we?
THOMAS HARDY

THE TRADITIONAL FARMHOUSES of England have not survived for hundreds of years because of their charming looks. The farmer did not aspire to the simple life and his choice of a home was guided by comfort, fashion and economy. If his picturesque thatch was no match for the spring gales or if a strategically placed chamber pot was required to catch the water every time it rained, he was unsentimental about seeking an affordable replacement for it.

During the seventeenth century, the farmers who visited Bridgwater in Somerset with the state of their thatch in mind were impressed by news of an admirable new roofing material. Dutch pantiles, traded for wool and fine English cloth at the port, were beginning to make their mark on the houses of the town. Soon they were being shipped inland along the waterways and used to replace the mouldering thatch on the farms and houses which lay close by. Although the old roofs took a new cover, many kept the steep pitch more suited to thatch. Eventually, the demand for pantiles outstripped supply and in the eighteenth century, when a local entrepreneur started to manufacture and market Bridgwater's own pantile, flat in the middle and rolled at either end, the pantile virtually replaced the thatch of the farmhouses of Avon and north Somerset.

The spread of the Bridgwater tile demonstrates how habits change. The vernacular style, which gradually died out with the advent of cheap, mass-produced building materials, was always subject to the

LEFT: MOORLAND AND VALLEY
Earth and stone characterize the traditional farmhouses of the west country. From the sandstones of the east and the cob of the central region to the granite and slate of the west, farmhouses like this one near Porthmeor in Cornwall were made from what the builder found beneath his feet.

LEFT: BRIDGWATER PANTILES
Brandish Street Farm near Allerford in Somerset may have had a thatched roof at one time. Pantiles, shipped into the port at Bridgwater during the seventeenth century and carried inland along the waterways, created a local demand for the new material. Eventually, Bridgwater manufactured its own tiles.

dictates of comfort and fashion and the people of the west country were not slow to adopt ideas from outside. Yet the south-west has retained a rich stock of traditional buildings: more cob and thatch exists in the west today than in the rest of the country put together and Cornwall still possesses the greatest concentration of granite buildings. These were essentially the product of the Great Rebuilding which flowered in the west during the sixteenth and seventeenth centuries. The fact that so many cob and granite buildings have survived for 300 and 400 years is a testimony to the inherent practicability of the local styles. Despite maverick materials like the Bridgwater pantile, the traditionally designed farmhouse clearly served the farmers of Avon, Somerset, Dorset, Devon and Cornwall as well as the surrounding land did.

The land is broadly divided between the lush and languid east and the stern and exposed west. From the farmer's point of view, the west was separated by the geographical boundary between upland and lowland, the highland zone characterized by the bleak open scenery of Bodmin Moor, Dartmoor and Exmoor, the lowland by fertile vales like Taunton Deane between the Quantock Hills and Blackdown Hills, the meadowlands of the Frome and Stour and the wet, wide expanse of the Somerset levels.

The twentieth-century tendency for farmers to specialize and the consequent surpluses of products like milk and wheat has led to demands for farmers to diversify. In both the highland and lowland areas of the west country, the lie of the land had long dictated a mixed economy; on the heathered hills of Dartmoor or down among the clefted coastline valleys and wooded vales, conventional farming was regularly supplemented by other sources of income. The opportunistic farming community added pigs, poultry and anything else their labour could generate to a predominantly pastoral economy, based upon the stocky Red Devon cow and the fat Dorset Horn sheep. The farmer might raise a few Dartmoor ponies bred for the packhorse trade or plant a cider orchard on a field fertilized with rotten fish. Some scraped the skin off their backs mining copper and tin at St Just, Cornwall, or working the coalfields at Radstock in Avon; others dug china clay on Bodmin Moor or peat bricks near Glastonbury. They

RIGHT: CLASSICAL PORCH
Farms in Dorset, Devon, Somerset and Avon were founded on fertile ground and many farmhouses were correspondingly large and prosperous. This ornate two-storey porch would have been added to Hammoon Manor (opposite) as a fashionable afterthought.

RIGHT: HAMMOON MANOR
A thatch of barn-like dimensions encompasses the roof of this grand manor at Hammoon in Dorset, a building which is over four hundred years old.

made cheddar cheese from the milk yields of cattle grazed on the Somerset levels and wicker baskets from the plantations of willow that grew there.

The Cornishman who hoed and harrowed by day might spend his nights in a crab boat or in shifting and storing the significant quantities of contraband which were being beached under the cover of darkness during the eighteenth century. Even the intermittent looting of shipwrecks provided a welcome windfall. As one priest put it: 'We pray, O Lord, not that wrecks should occur, but that if they do, Thou wilt drive them into the Scilly Isles for the benefit of the poor inhabitants.'

Many of these enterprises have their archaeological evidence in the little sheds, cellars and outhouses tacked on to the side of the farmer's home or built out in the yard. On the Somerset levels, some farmers had a boatshed to store the flat-bottomed craft used when the land flooded; in the Devon farmyard there might be a two-storey linhay where stock was housed on the ground floor and hay stacked

RIGHT: CHAPEL WINDOW
Stone, fashioned like flower petals, created the framework for this small, circular window in what was a private chapel at Woolbridge Manor.

RIGHT: WOOLBRIDGE MANOR
The seventeenth-century manor at Wool in Dorset has undergone several renovations, including a partial reroofing in clay tiles. Woolbridge Manor was used by Thomas Hardy as one of the settings in Tess of the d'Urbervilles.

above. Then there was the conical ash house which stored the household's wood and peat ash before it was spread on the fields as fertilizer, the laity or milk house, the brewhouse, the cool store for cheeses or smoked fish and a lean-to which sheltered the carts, the poultry and the farmyard cats. Like the farmhouse itself, each was built from what lay beneath its foundations. Since the ground stones ranged from limestone to granite, their outward appearance possessed as much uniformity as hat styles at Ascot.

The geological map of the south-west is patterned with swirling rock formations. In the west, granites and associated igneous rocks like porphyry, polyphant and catacleuse are marooned in a sea of shales, sandstones and clays. Old red sandstones, triassic marls, lias and greensands ooze out of the east to meet and mingle with them.

In the east where the limestone belt finally petered out, stone-masons took the local stone no further than its natural borders for it weathered badly the further north it travelled. Where the limestone was used on the farms and farm buildings, it varied from the mellow

LEFT: FRONT CHIMNEY
Placing the chimney stack on the front of the house was a common practice in western areas. Often, an additional flue was linked to the chimney to create a bacon-curing chamber beside the hearth.

LEFT: THATCH AND LIMEWASH
The west country farmer relied on a mixed agricultural economy and the farmhouse had to serve as a working building. Homes such as this one at Bossington in Somerset would have housed the bakehouse, brewery and dairy as well as the farming family.

ABOVE: STONE POST
Throughout the south-west, the variety of building stone is striking. This ornamental post, carved in limestone, has itself become decorated with lichens.

Yellow Lias, or Ham Hill stone of Somerset, to the Blue Lias (lias being a corruption of the quarryman's term 'layers') which was more grey than blue. In Somerset, Blue Lias gave a slightly sombre look to the farms around Somerton; while the fine-grained Ham Hill stone put as tight a finish on the ashlar walls of old farms around Martock and Montacute as on any Cotswold mansion. Like the oolitic limestones of the Cotswolds, it could be sawn into lintels and split into roofing slates and its tendency to provide a footing for lichens gave the buildings the natural look of a weathered bed of stone.

Sandstones also appeared in every conceivable colour and quality. There were the greensands, soft enough to form ashlar walls on farmhouses scattered along the Somerset and Dorset border between Chard and Lyme Regis, and new red sandstones which warmed the village walls near Exmoor, the Quantocks and the Brendon Hills. On the hills themselves, the farms were built of the hard grey Devonian rocks. Interleaved between the greensands of south-west Somerset and east Devon were bands of chert, used by neolithic tool-makers as

RIGHT: EAST STOKE FARM
The fine quality of the local limestone in this part of Somerset allowed the mason to cut and dress the stone to give a shadow-free finish to the face of this farm at Stoke Sub Hamdon.

LEFT: ROLLING THATCH
With its shuttered windows, cobbled path and neat thatch tightly rolled over the dormer windows, this agricultural building at Stoke Sub Hamdon in Somerset may have once housed farmworkers.

a substitute for flint, and by the farmer to form coursed stonework between quoins of greensand or brick. Yet another sandstone, dark brown this time, outcropped west of Dartmoor where the old horse bridge which crossed the Tamar between Sydenham Damerel and Stoke Climsland was built of it.

However, more mud than stone was used to build the farmhouses of the mid-south-west. Mud, mixed with chopped straw and a little lime to aid the setting process, is the cob of the west country, the basic building material which gave the farmer a house which was both cool in summer and warm in winter. The practice of building from the raw earth is, if not as old as the hills, then as old as the first people to seek shelter beneath them. The farmers who built in cob knew their soil. They knew when it was ready for the seed drill and when it was in a fit state to be formed into the farmhouse walls.

ABOVE: BASCLOSE FARM
The chequerboard effect of building this lateral or front chimney in two different types of stone makes it a prominent feature of the longhouse (right). It also serves to protect the soft, brown sandstone from erosion.

To build in cob, a foundation plinth of stone, tarred against the damp, was laid down and then layered with cob made from a stiff sludge of straw and mud: one Devon 'recipe' called for nine cartloads of clay mixed with one load of barley straw, while the Cornish version, known as clob, was likely to have broken slate added to the mix. Each layer, three to four feet wide, was tamped down on its foundations and left to dry for a week or two before the next layer was added. Corners were rounded for better stability (moreover, the superstitious insisted that a rounded corner afforded the devil no hiding-place) and windows, doorframes and floor joists were put in as the building slowly rose. Paring irons, used to cut away any excess material, left tell-tale slice marks on the walls which were finished with a layer of protective plaster and a coat of white, cream or even blue limewash. On farm buildings where the cob was occasionally

RIGHT: SMITH HILL FARM
Where the farmer chose to settle in the pastoral uplands of a place like Dartmoor, the farmhouse, like this one near Two Bridges, was tucked down into a sheltered site.

LEFT: EARTH WORKS
Wet clay and straw laid in layers over a stone plinth was the basic method of construction for the cob houses of the west country. This cob longhouse, Basclose Farm at Otterton in Devon was built in the seventeenth century. Thatch, needed no heavy roof timbers and provided the ideal hat for a house of earth.

RIGHT: SHOULDERED PORCH
The longhouse doorway had to be wide enough to admit the horned cattle and, according to some farmers, a hogshead of cider. This porch is at Sanders in Lettaford, Devon.

ABOVE: HARD CHOICE
Granite was never an easy stone to work, but the geology of Dartmoor offered the builder no better stone. Capped with slate, the central chimney at Sanders farm demonstrates the mason's skills.

left bare, the walls were soon pitted and pockmarked by browsing cattle and nesting insects, but provided they were protected with a coping of thatch, they lasted well enough. Thatch, sufficiently lightweight not to bear down too heavily on the walls, was the ideal roof covering for the farmhouse as well.

A chimney of stone or brick was built into the walls, typically positioned on the front elevation beside the door, frequently with a rounded bread oven built into its base. On some farms, two extra flues were added to the chimney, one leading to a bacon-smoking oven, the other to a scalding oven for making clotted cream.

The dimensions of the farmhouse depended on the size and fertility of the holding and although cob is usually associated with the smaller two-storey, four-roomed cottage, it was used on substantial farmhouses such as Hayes Barton in Devon, the birthplace of Sir Walter Raleigh. Raleigh shared the west countryman's fondness for the cob house. 'I had rather see myself there than anywhere else,' he wrote, despite having visited more corners of the globe than most people in the seventeenth century.

The farmhouses of cob and stone so far described were lowland farms, built among rich grazing grounds and cider orchards which sent snowdrifts of blossom across the countryside in spring and filled the chill air of autumn with the smell of fermenting apples. The farms, rarely as ostentatious as those in the south and east, nevertheless added their own decorative details to the farmyard scene, like the farmyard pump, housed beneath its own thatched roof, or the year date carved over a door built wide enough to admit a hogshead of cider.

In contrast, the highland farms were spartan, self-contained and remote. The moors, where many were built, were more heavily populated in the eighteenth and nineteenth centuries than they are today and old tracks which pick their way between the peat bogs invariably arrive at a muddle of strewn stone which was once a farming family's home. However barren or inhospitable the landscape, there is invariably some evidence of settlement: a barn of rounded boulders with windows like arrow slits; a deserted fisherman's cottage constructed of sea-washed slabs; a grey granite

ABOVE: SYMPATHETIC RESTORATION
There are no longer any longhouses on Dartmoor which shelter the farmer and his animals. The stonework and windows of the shippon at Sanders, renovated by the Landmark Trust, have been restored to their original condition.

longhouse high up among the tors; or a quarryman's croft, its parapeted gables shouldering up to a rough roof long ago robbed of its slate.

A lack of good freestone or timber meant that cowhouse and farm rose in the same rough, intractable stone as the hill tops, and kept a rugged harmony with their surroundings. In the latter part of the Middles Ages when masons learnt to use pitchers, chisels and punches to dress off the granite, the house walls took on an even, if rough-hewn, look. Eventually, hand saws capable of cutting granite would produce sawn stone to dress the farmhouse walls, but on the early buildings the builder simply levered stones out of a cliff face or rolled moor stones on to the site of the house. Occasionally, a particularly large boulder served as a key stone, the rest of the house being constructed around its immovable bulk.

House and barn were customarily built as one low, horizon-hugging dwelling, the longhouse. More were erected on and around Dartmoor in the sixteenth and seventeenth centuries than anywhere else in England and, when they ceased making them in Devon during

ABOVE: FRAGILE FOOTING
Fern and flower find a foothold in the brick and flint garden wall which surrounds Hayes Barton at East Budleigh.

RIGHT: HAYES BARTON
Cob was being used in Devon during the thirteenth century and the county still possesses more cob buildings than any other. Hayes Barton was built of cob shortly before Sir Walter Raleigh was born here in 1552. It is a large E-shaped farmhouse.

LEFT: DAIRY FARM
Devon cream came from Devon cows and most farmers possessed a milking herd. Farmyards were often enclosed by other buildings and the covered entrance, seen here at Hayes Barton, needed to be sufficiently high to admit a cart loaded with hay or corn.

the seventeenth century, the longhouse continued to be built in the north and the Midlands. The floor plan of the basic longhouse was simple: a single living room on the one end, the animal quarters or byre on the other. The byre was set downhill of the house and a cross-passage, running between house and byre, led through the building from front to back. The doorway, wide enough to admit the cattle, was shared by the farmer and his animals, although by the late seventeenth century most farmers had constructed a separate house entrance with a rainproof porch above it.

Windows, if the cottage possessed them, were mere pig's eye-holes in the walls, closed with a fixed pane of glass if they were lucky, a sheet of oiled cloth and a shutter if they were not—the stone chimney could let in more light than the windows. But the highland farmer was not immune to the seventeenth-century rise in living standards. The single living room was partitioned off into kitchen and bedchamber and a loft bedroom or store, reached by a ladder, was built into the attic. New windows were let into the walls and a workshop for

RIGHT: COB AND STONE
When it was built in the eighteenth century, the symmetrical proportions of Trenow near Gulval in Cornwall looked fashionably correct. However, a cowshed and barn, reached from the back of the farmhouse, are concealed behind one pair of windows.

RIGHT: RURAL INDUSTRY
Cornwall was one of the foremost producers of tin and copper in the eighteenth and nineteenth centuries. Many miners supplemented their family incomes by keeping a few head of cattle or sheep, stalled at night in some granite outhouse.

LEFT: ELEMENTAL PROTECTION
The stern nature of Cornish granite contrasts with the rounded features of Devon cob, but this rugged stone played its part in keeping the westerly winds and rain at bay. The double-storey porch on Tregarden near St Mabyn gave extra protection from the weather.

BELOW: LEADED LIGHTS
Traditional windows like these at Tregarden were kept small and set back in the stone. Stormy weather discouraged the use of generously sized windows. The small window on the right lit the farmer's hat room.

spinning or butter making was added to the gable end or back of the house. Even in the nineteenth century, it was not unusual for a family of eight or more to be living in these crowded conditions and, when he could afford to do so, the farmer would add a second storey to the house and perhaps build an extra room over the porch. Later still, the cattle were moved to a separate barn and the old byre was incorporated into the house.

Having to heave a loft ladder off the upper floor every time the occupants wanted to ascend or descend was an awkward inconvenience and a winding, stone stairway was put in, often tucked into the wall beside the fireplace. The stout, sometimes rounded chimney which rose above the fireplace withstood these winds of change, although the rough thatch or turf covering on the roof below gradually gave way to a chain-mail of Cornish slate. Parapets, roughly built like the house wall and run down the slope of the thatched gable, tended to disappear beneath the replacement roof for in the south-west there was no shortage of slate.

BELOW: TREGARDEN
'By Tre, Pol and Pen,/ You shall know Cornishmen.' There has been a recent resurgence of interest in the Cornish language which virtually died out in the eighteenth century. 'Tre' is Cornish for a homestead or hamlet.

BELOW: CORNISH COTTAGES
Slate has been quarried in Cornwall for over six hundred years. The blue-grey stone was used not only to roof buildings like these at Porthmeor, but also for farm floors, lintels and drinking troughs.

When violent seismic eruptions squeezed and baked the shales and mudstones of Cumbria, North Wales and Cornwall, they turned into great, grey seams of slate. By the time Sir Walter Raleigh was chivalrously laying his cloak across a puddle in front of Elizabeth I, the slate was already being quarried in Cornwall. Small quarries were also opened in Devon, but at Delabole near Camelford workers were excavating what would become the biggest quarry in England, one and a half miles round and 500 feet deep. Slate was tough, waterproof and impervious to frost and made as much of a mark around the farm as on the farmhouse roof: slate paved the dairy floor and provided

RIGHT: EMPTY FARMHOUSE
The hill farmer had to contend with poor grazing and distant markets to make a living. Sometimes the fight for survival defeated the farmer and the old farmhouse was abandoned.

BELOW: CORNISH COTTAGES
Slate has been quarried in Cornwall for over six hundred years. The blue-grey stone was used not only to roof buildings like these at Porthmeor, but also for farm floors, lintels and drinking troughs.

LEFT: HILLSBOROUGH FARM
Joints in the slate-hung walls of Hillsborough Farm near Boscastle in Cornwall have been mortared together for extra weather protection. The farmhouse roof was slurried with cement mortar for the same reason.

the slabs where the cheese was made; it served as drinking troughs for the cattle and, laid in a pleasing herringbone fashion, walled the kitchen garden against them; salt-troughs, lintels, steps, window sills and kitchen floors were all made with slate and, when the old farmer died, a slab of slate in the graveyard recorded his passing.

The Cornish quarries poured out neat rectangles of greenish roofing slate, their size obscurely related to the female upper classes so that a typical order would include Queens, Princesses, Duchesses, Marchionesses and Countesses. In north-west Devon the thicker, rougher 'rag' slates were used, but the Cornish farmer preferred what were simply called 'peggies', small, neat slates which hung by an oak peg on the roof battens. Until the nineteenth century, Cornwall had more slate-roofed farmhouses than any other English region outside Cumbria: mile for contorted mile, it probably possessed more coastline too. The coast, as the local people put it, saw a bit of weather and granite was the preferred material to meet it. Quays, breakwaters and embankments were all formed in granite, as were whole villages like Polperro or Cadgwith on the Lizard peninsula where the local granite gave a greeny-red colour to the farmhouse walls. At Cadgwith, the thatched roofs of the pink and white cottages were held down with heavy chains; elsewhere the slate roofs of the coast were slurried with cement and sometimes doubly secured with wires run over the roof from one side to the other to keep out the westerly winds. For the same reason, the windward side of seaside farmhouses was often hung with slate.

The Cornish seaboard is dotted with small ports and harbours which in the eighteenth and nineteenth centuries shipped out considerable quantities of slate, exports which contributed to the gradual disappearance of the thatched and stone-flagged roofs of England. The West Country is a land of small farms, many of which have remained in the hands of the same families for generations. These were farmers who held fast to traditional customs and who have avoided radically altering their own houses for several hundred years. Given a new roof of thatch and a fresh coat or two of limewash, the good looks of the west country farmhouses should survive for another century or so.

ABOVE: PROTECTED FUTURE
Many of the western farmhouses have stood the test of time over three or four centuries. Given this slate protection, they have a secure future.

CHAPTER FOUR

MIDDLE ENGLAND

Ay, the horses trample,
The harness jingles now;
No change though you lie under
The land you used to plough.
A. E. HOUSMAN

DESPITE HIS REPUTATION for conservatism, the farmer is no stranger to change. However, since Housman's death in 1936, the pace of change has acquired the momentum of a tornado with the eye of the storm centred on middle England.

As the Industrial Revolution spread through the coal-rich heart of England, rural labourers quit their cottages for the brick back-to-backs of the city. When the grim realities of urban life crowded in on these former landworkers, the hardships they had suffered on the land mellowed into memories: pictures of country life showing the wagoner's boy watering his horses or village women gleaning the fields were hung in tenements to remind them of their past.

The farmers meanwhile doubled and redoubled their efforts to meet the demand for their produce. Fields were enlarged, common land was enclosed and the plough put to previously unploughed land. Within a generation, the cheap prints of the old countryside depicted a way of life which had become redundant. The wagoner's boy and the shire horse, jangling its collar brasses against the evil eye, were finally beaten by the tractor; the hay rick and straw stack were replaced by the utilitarian tin barn; hedgerows and old woods were grubbed up and the elm tree, once such a potent feature of the English horizon, took ill and died. The one constant element in the changing landscape of middle England was the traditional farmhouse.

LEFT: DEMESNE
The farmhouses of middle England are the one constant element in a changing countryside. Demesne Farm at Garway in Herefordshire lies in the Monnow valley with the Black Mountains of the Welsh Marches in the distance. The demesne was the farm and land held by the manor.

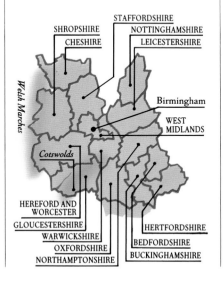

LEFT: COLD NEWTON

The nineteenth-century datestone over the porch of this Leicestershire farmhouse almost certainly denotes the year it was improved. This Cold Newton farm is older than it appears.

Middle England embraces thirteen shires: Cheshire, Nottinghamshire, Shropshire, Staffordshire, Leicestershire, Hereford and Worcester, Warwickshire, Northamptonshire, Gloucestershire, Oxfordshire, Buckinghamshire, Bedfordshire and Hertfordshire. Since geological variety in these central counties is nowhere surpassed in the other regions, the range of farmhouse designs is equally diverse.

The central and most memorable feature of the geology is where the limestone belt, running the 300 miles from Dorset to Humberside, intersects middle England. Passing through Gloucestershire, Oxfordshire, Northamptonshire and Leicestershire, it produced a classic stone. To the east of the limestone, beyond a ribbon of greensand and gault, lies a band of chalk which wells up in Wiltshire and runs, parallel with the limestone, into eastern England. Interspersed in the chalk are pockets of clay and sand dumped by receding glaciers during the last Ice Age. The older rock formations lie to the west of the limestone belt: the millstone grits of the Staffordshire borders, the dark red and yellow sandstones of the West Midlands,

LEFT: RICH DIVERSITY

The richly varied geology of middle England resulted in a spectacular diversity of farmhouse style and design. This building at Blakesley in Northamptonshire exhibits the use of a pliable stone which was as easily cut to form mullions for the windows as it was built into the warm, brown walls of the farmhouse.

the pale red sandstone of Shropshire and, in the north-west, the grassy marls and clays which fatten the Cheshire dairy herds.

Each and every one of these rock formations has made some mark on the face of farmhouses. Seen through the eyes of the eighteenth-century cattle drovers, cutting across the region from west to east, the farmhouses revealed an almost limitless variety of vernacular styles. The drovers reckoned to cross from North Wales to Kent in three weeks, avoiding main roads and costly toll gates as they made their noisy way past the whitewashed longhouses of Wales, the rough stone and shale cottages of the borders, the fine yellow stone of the Cotswold farms, the thatch and rubble stone of Oxfordshire, the brick and tile of Buckinghamshire and the white, plastered or weatherboarded farms of Hertfordshire. From the sheep-cropped hills of Shropshire to the fertile vales of the Trent valley and from the Herefordshire hop yards to the Thames valley grain fields, the drovers met with every kind of farmer growing for every kind of market. Driving before them their ponderous cattle, wandering sheep and even flocks of turkeys, their feet tarred for the journey, the drovers passed through the buffer zone between the pastoral upland

ABOVE: AIR VENTS
Built on a plinth of local stone, the half-timbered walls of the great barn at Cosby House in Leicestershire were constructed with gaps in the brickwork to allow fresh air to circulate around the stooks of corn stored inside.

RIGHT: COSBY HOUSE BARN
William Morris considered some country barns to be 'as beautiful as a cathedral'. The interior of this Leicestershire barn, with dove-holes in the gables and pegged timberwork, confirms his opinion.

LEFT: ARTFUL CRAFT
Gate locks, like farmhouses, vary from region to region and from parish to parish. The blacksmith who created this device for a Leicestershire farmer put as much art as craft into his work.

MIND STEP

ABOVE: BOTTLE GLASS WINDOW

An early window, glazed with leaded panes, lights the upper floor of a double-storey porch. Until the fifteenth century, glazed windows were the prerogative of the rich. The poor had to make do with a sheet of oiled linen cloth or thin slivers of cattle horn instead of glass.

LEFT: GREEN DOOR

Wrought iron strap hinges, probably cast by the local smithy, decorate the front door at Deverell's Farm in Swanbourne, Buckinghamshire.

farming of the west and the arable plains of the east. The villagers watched their progress with suspicion and when the dust had settled and the sound of the drovers' corgis had faded into the distance, they hurriedly checked their own stock for missing animals. Three villages, Longtown, Bibury and Haddenham serve to illustrate the wide regional differences.

Longtown is a remote Marches village overlooked by the glowering Black Mountains where curlews call in the spring and buzzards quarter a landscape of small fields and grazing commons. The sixteenth- and seventeenth-century farmhouses with their stone walls and stone-flagged roofs nestled down in the valleys, took wide, double-storeyed porches against the elements and, in the longhouse tradition, kept a cowshed or barn on their downhill side. Eighteenth-century field and farm names like the Hopyard, Orchard and Tanhouse suggest an earlier more mixed economy than the present one which rests almost exclusively on the solid backs of mountain cattle and sheep.

LEFT: DEVERELL'S FARM
The local stone used on this farmhouse is complemented by an undulating roof of small clay tiles, parapetted gables ending in kneeler stones and an elegant, central brick chimney.

Bibury, by contrast, was founded on the fourteenth-century sheep trade. This Gloucestershire village, claimed by the arch-exponent of the Arts and Crafts Movement, William Morris, to be the most beautiful village in England, wears a mantle of cool Cotswold limestone. The village and its surrounding farms experienced a second upturn in their fortunes in the early seventeenth century when the farmers and cottagers took to weaving. Today most of the neighbouring pastures are deep ploughed for arable use and race horses, rather than sheep, graze its grass.

The third scene is radically different, for the whitewashed walls of Haddenham in Buckinghamshire were built not of stone but of earth. A century ago, the good wives of the parish would have sat in their doorways, plucking and feathering their prized Haddenham ducks and looking across at the neighbouring farms of wichert and thatch. Like Devon cob, wichert was another highly localized method of building with raw earth. Constructing a mud house capable of surviving the average wet, English winter seems as doomed a project

LEFT: HAYWOOD LODGE
Set in the rich Herefordshire countryside, the symmetrical facade of this Queen Anne house conceals a complex of barns, cowsheds and brick hop kilns behind. Originally built to serve as a forest lodge for the hunting bishops of Hereford, Haywood Lodge was later turned into a working farm.

LEFT: GREAT TURNANT
Like so many farms along the Marches borderland, this hill farm has been in the hands of the same family for several generations. Built in sandstone under the brooding Black Mountains, the walls of the farmhouse were once whitewashed.

as building a sandcastle below the high tide line but, given a damp-proof base, a sheltering roof and a strong surface protection, these houses of clay have already outlived the muddied builder by a dozen generations and more. Wichert, a layer of hard earth and yellow ochre chalk which lies just below ground level, covers an area of six square miles around Haddenham. The earth was made into a wet, glutinous mix, reinforced with small stones, straw and reed and then trodden into walling layers over a base of chalk blocks. Since each layer had to harden before the next was laid, wichert was a slow process. A surface coat of lime plaster protected and concealed the farmhouse walls, although yard and garden walls, capped with a hat of thatch or pantiles, were left bare.

Stone and wichert were by no means the only materials employed on the farmhouses of middle England. There were the magpied, half-timbered houses of the west, the cheerful red brick of the east, the mellowed limestone of the south and the dark brick and stone of the north. The vernacular styles of middle England were dictated by local geology and topography: what lay beneath the builder's feet, or grew in his backyard, was generally what went into the fabric of the farmhouse. Like Haddenham, each shire had its own maverick designs which appear in one parish and disappear in the next. One farmhouse in the Forest of Dean was close enough to the local iron works to have been constructed in black blocks of furnace slag; another in Shropshire boasts an unusual amount of metalwork with iron lintels, window frames, doorsteps and chimney pots, all brought from nearby foundries at Coalbrookdale. Yet another, built close to the derelict remains of some borderland castle, has robbed the ruin of its best building stone; while a fourth, on the banks of the navigable River Severn, is built of old brick and pantiles, the result of some discreet trade between a farmer and a bargee. These anomalies make it difficult to generalize about the farmhouses of middle England, although oak, limestone and brick provided the dominant building materials.

Clay was being moulded into bricks and fired to a weatherproofed hardness when the Romans colonized middle England. The Roman *tegula* was a long, thin brick developed to act as a tie for walls of flint

ABOVE: COTSWOLD STONE
A belt of limestone runs across the country from Dorset to Humberside. Where it passed through the Cotswolds, the local stone, seen here at Great Coxwell barn (opposite) was used for roofs as well as walls.

or rubble while the English brick, first made in the brickyards of East Anglia, was half its length and four times its thickness. Almost two thousand years later, it had become the basic building unit for the Industrial Revolution and such an excess of brick gave the material a bad name. However, the old brickwork of Nottinghamshire, Leicestershire, southern Bedfordshire, Hertfordshire and Buckinghamshire exhibits a more sympathetic use of the material.

Where clay was plentiful and the farmhouse in need of repair or rebuilding, the clay was dug, moulded and fired on site. In the farmyard clamp, unfired or green bricks were cased in clay and stacked over a base of fired bricks and firewood. At a controlled 900 degrees centigrade, the iron in brick clay burns through the brick to produce a uniform red, while a fiercer heat produces purples, dark reds and browns. But these temporary brickyards and their makeshift kilns, open to the elements, turned out bricks which displayed an individuality quite absent from the regular, machine-made brick. Underfired bricks were saved for internal use; overfired and vitrified bricks might be reserved to produce a chequered pattern along the eaves or around doors and windows. When the job was finished, the brick pit would fill with water and serve as a duck pond—nothing went to waste.

Until the mid-sixteenth century, brickwork was confined to the more affluent farmhouses east of an imaginary line between the Solent and the Humber, partly because these areas lacked good building stone and partly because Flemish ideas on brickwork were still filtering slowly across the country from the eastern ports. On smaller, stone-built farmhouses, brickwork was introduced to form fireproof chimneys, door arches, or outhouses for the dairy and brewhouse. The wattle and daub on the timber-framed farms of Warwickshire and Worcestershire was gradually replaced with horizontal or herringbone brick noggings, while in parts of Leicestershire and the Thames valley, brick became the dominant walling material. Whether on the upper waters of the Trent, where the bricks and tiles were drawn from the locally abundant Trias clays, or in the Vale of Gloucester, where bricks formed great gable end chimney stacks, the dusty red or dark purple bricks looked right and proper.

RIGHT: GREAT COXWELL BARN
Great Coxwell, near Faringdon in Oxfordshire, was built for Cistercian monks between 1275 and 1325, and is now in the hands of the National Trust. The inspiration for the traditional designs of Cotswold farmhouses came from the way limestone was used on buildings like this.

LEFT: VERSATILE STONE

The pliable limestone which formed the farmhouse walls could be split into roofing slates, built into field walls or shaped into the mushroom-shaped staddle stones seen here at Great Coxwell.

LEFT: REJUVENATION

Most of the thriving village of Pickworth in Leicestershire was mysteriously abandoned at the end of the thirteenth century, although this single arch of the medieval church has survived. Cut stone taken from the old church would have been used by the resourceful farmer in the building of his farmhouse.

The homogenous look of farm buildings in the Cotswolds, like these at Duntisbourne Leer in Gloucestershire, is due partly to the plentiful supply of local stone and partly to conservative traditions which lasted far longer than in neighbouring areas.

Until the first brick tax was introduced in 1784, the demand for bricks outstripped supplies. Fly-by-night brickmakers set up temporary kilns on village greens, digging the clay and baking and selling bricks by the roadside until irate commoners drove them away. Even the succession of prohibitive brick taxes did not halt production as the ingenious brickmaker found loopholes in the law, first by making a clay 'block' which was a double-sized brick, and later by moulding the lightweight brick tile which proved so popular in the south-east.

Little brickwork existed in the central limestone belt where the farmers possessed such an abundance of fine-grained oolitic limestone, they could dispense with hedges and mark out their newly enclosed pastures with stone cleared from the fields. Most villages possessed a local quarry and each produced a stone of a different quality and colour to its neighbour. Some, like Taynton quarry, noted in the Domesday book as a valuable resource, was already used in Saxon times. The stone, fresh from the quarry, was as easily sawn into neat building blocks as it was worked into mushroom-shaped staddle stones, used to support the granary and keep out rats and mice. With a material as versatile as this, the Cotswold farmhouse exhibited decorative details which a down-to-earth Yorkshireman would have condemned as unnecessarily fussy; roofs, stone slated and sharply pitched, ran up alongside steep parapets finished with a finial or tall chimney; secondary gables, each with a central window to light the bedchamber, were built into the roofline; stone-mullioned windows with their wrought-iron frames were set deep in a groove in the stone; elaborate drip stones were moulded above the windows. On poorer holdings, the details were kept simple— wooden lintels, for example, were used in place of carved drip moulds and small dormers instead of grand gabled windows.

The Cotswold tradition has a lineage which reaches back into the Middle Ages, to the days when the land was held by the great religious communities who built their cathedral-like tithe barns at Great Coxwell, Bredon, Frocester and Hartpury. These medieval warehouses stored the tithe, or tenth, of parishioners' crops, paid as a tax to the monasteries who between them owned about a quarter of the landed wealth of England at the time of their dissolution in 1538.

The Cotswold farmers, enjoying the wealth of the wool trade in the fourteenth and fifteenth centuries, had money enough to spend on new homes. Their builders borrowed from the Gothic style of these monastic buildings and as a result produced an homogeneous building style, based on medieval building techniques and preserved by conservative tradition far later than in adjoining counties. The effect of so much natural stone on the limestone landscape ensured that the farmhouses and outbuildings were comfortably assimilated into the surrounding countryside.

The Great Rebuilding reached these areas in the late seventeenth century and resulted in the rebuilding of smaller farmhouses and cottages, many of them financed by the wool-weaving industry—the presence of long, open attic rooms lit by dormer windows on the upper storeys of some Cotswold farms suggests that the practice of weaving and farming went hand in hand as it did in northern England. Another source of income came from 'ridding', the business of taking new stone from the local quarry and laying it out to be seasoned by the winter weather. After several hard frosts, the limestone could be split into thin roofing slates or thicker stone suitable for field walls which hedged in the stock and afforded some protection from the worst of the winter blizzards. The high villages of the Cotswolds are still the first in middle England to be cut off in a hard winter and farmhouses were sensibly set in sheltered valleys.

The Cotswold farmhouse with its sharp gables and graded slate roofs comes to an abrupt halt above the city of Gloucester where the limestone escarpment looks west towards the hills of the Welsh borders. These little mountains line the horizon, their silhouettes like a school of dolphins at play, while the fertile bowl of Hereford and Worcester, hop, cider-apple and market-garden country, laps at its feet. To the north, Long Mynd and the Clee Hills outcrop in Shropshire, the poorest agricultural region of the West Midlands. Beyond them, the Cheshire Plain lies cupped between the North Wales mountains, the Irish Sea and the tail of the Pennines.

This is a marginal countryside where the farmhouse is in transition from the Celtic longhouse to the Saxon hall house. To the south, tucked away among the oak and beech of the Forest of Dean, grey,

ABOVE: BLACK AND WHITE
The habit of blacking the timbers and whitewashing the panels on half-timbered buildings is the hallmark of the timber-framed farms of middle England. Some authorities attribute the habit of tarring the timbers to the Victorian age.

slatey farms give way to the old red sandstone of south Herefordshire. Then comes the spectacular swathe of half-timbered farmhouses running from Herefordshire through Worcestershire, Warwickshire, Shropshire and Cheshire.

The entire history of the half-timbered farmhouse can be traced in this sweep of border farmland. There was no shortage of oak in the rural West Midlands and most farmhouses displayed their timberwork with pride. The more southerly villages look like museum pieces, preserved to illustrate the early cruck- and later box-frame constructions with their plain panels and black painted oaks. Those of the north tend to be more decorative with flamboyant curves and criss-crosses, zigzags and quatrefoils set into the panels.

Oak is not inherently perishable. Left for long enough, it will harden to the saw-blunting texture of iron, and the ninth-century oaks in the half-timbered church at Greensted-juxta-Ongar in Essex are in no worse condition today than those in the sixteenth-century Little Moreton Hall in Cheshire. Occasionally, sound timbers taken

BELOW: LOWER BROCKHAMPTON
Despite their apparent similarities, each West Midlands half-timbered farmhouse is as distinctive as a fingerprint. This small window is set in the upper floor of the two-storey gatehouse (opposite), built across the moat which surrounded the manor house near Bromyard, Herefordshire.

RIGHT: REBUILDING
This farmhouse, now the property of the National Trust, was built in the fourteenth century and substantially rebuilt in the sixteenth and seventeenth centuries. The gatehouse dates from the fifteenth century.

BELOW: BARGEBOARDS
Bargeboards, carved with the popular medieval design of a trailing vine, not only provide a little ornamentation but protect projecting roof timbers from the weather. While the manor house here is roofed with small clay tiles, stone tiles have been used on the gatehouse (below left and opposite).

from some redundant building might be recycled, but the notion that old ships' timbers were used in the farmhouse is a fallacy. The traditional method of using oak (other hardwood has been used but English oak predominated) was to cut and work the wood while it was still green and soft. The trees selected for the farmhouse were stripped of bark where they stood in spring, the bark being sold to the tanning industry, and then felled ready for the start of the building season. (Records show that when the seventeenth-century carpenter, John Abel, undertook to restore a Cistercian abbey on the Herefordshire borders in 1632, his 204 tons of timber, purchased for five shillings a ton, were cut locally and used within months.) Seasoned wood was required only for wall panelling, doors, window frames, staircases and floorboards. The jigsaw of the framework was erected on site, the builders being guided by carpenters' marks, carved into the butt end of each beam, and indicating which mortise joint aligned with which tenon. Tapered oak pegs held the joints together and the exposed timberwork was left to season in place, the oaks weathering down to their natural silver-grey colour. The panels were filled with small wood and mud, and given a protective coat of limewash which had to be regularly reapplied as the timbers expanded and contracted, forming gaps between the wood and the wattle and daub.

The fashion for blacking the timbers is usually blamed on the Victorians, although restoration work on at least one early seventeenth-century, half-timbered building has exposed several layers of paint, including one of a bright sky-blue colour. The panels themselves may have been decorated with floral patterns and border designs—there is no reason to suppose the house owners of 300 years ago were any less colour conscious than today. Certainly the farmers of Cheshire liked to make a show of what could be done by a landowner with a well-lined pocket and a fondness for his region's traditions, and buildings like Morphany Hall and Little Moreton Hall make an extravagant display of timberwork between the panels.

The look of these fine and fashionable farmhouses has left a lasting impression on the borderland countryside. Their elaborate construction also made local heroes of master carpenters like Richard Dale,

RIGHT: MOAT FARM
Tiled weatherings, set over the first and second floors of this seventeenth-century farmhouse at Dormston in Worcestershire, are another feature peculiar to the half-timbered farmhouses of the West Midlands. Although they add to the maintenance work of the building, they protect the panels of wattle and daub from the rain.

MIDDLE ENGLAND

LEFT: FINE DISPLAY
Many of the half-timbered farmhouses in middle England were modest, two-storey buildings, but where the holding was large enough and the farm prosperous, the owner could afford to construct a house which was the envy of the neighbourhood, such as Leys Farm.

BELOW: LEYS FARM
Pargeting, the practice of decorating exterior plaster while it is still wet, is rarely found outside eastern and southern England. This detail of Leys Farm near Weobley is an unusual example.

who had worked on Little Moreton Hall, and Herefordshire's John Abel, described by Sir William Addison as 'the greatest of all the post-medieval architects in timber'.

The half-timbered farmhouses of the West Midlands led to a nineteenth-century rash of counterfeits with otherwise plain brick buildings being painted black and white in a manner which mocked their mimicry. However, both the border farmhouse and the graceful gabled Cotswold farmhouse were to make a significant contribution to the domestic buildings of the twentieth century. When the architects of the Tudor revival and the Arts and Crafts Movement began planning the pre- and post-war semis of the city suburbs, they drew inspiration from these vernacular designs. As we shall see in the next chapter, the look of the traditional farmhouses of northern England was also to be exported to the new garden suburbs being built in the south.

BELOW: NATURAL COLOUR
Where the oak timbers were left to season without a coat of paint, the wood, hardening to the texture of iron, took on a silver-grey look.

CHAPTER FIVE

NORTHERN ENGLAND

. . . bright, fierce and fickle is the South,
And dark and true and tender is the North.
ALFRED, LORD TENNYSON

T HE NORTH OF ENGLAND as Lord Tennyson suggests, is refreshingly different. From the base of its Pennine spine to the Cheviot foothills, the northern character is expressed in the regional dialects, the vernacular buildings and the landscapes. These landscapes are dramatic: the broad sweep of a Yorkshire vale, its litter of grey field barns chained to one another by a maze of drystone walls; the pot-holed cleft of a Pennine gorge plunging down to some clear-watered stream; the snow-wiped Cumbrian fell with a lonely, black-slate farmhouse at its foot.

For our purposes, the north begins in Derbyshire's Peak District, described by the eighteenth-century commentator Daniel Defoe as 'perhaps the most desolate, wild and abandoned country in all England'. From the Peaks, the Pennines march northwards through South, West and North Yorkshire. In the west, the mouth of Morecambe Bay separates the Lancashire plains from the abrupt eruption of the Cumbrian Mountains; in the east, the fertile lowlands of Lincolnshire and Humberside give way to the open fells of the North Yorkshire Moors and pass on into the broad hills of Durham and Northumberland.

At the local level, buildings and scenery are very different. The brown gritstone of a Derbyshire farmhouse with its heavy strap-pointing and burnt-sienna roof has little in common with the lamp-black slate roof and cheerful, painted face of a lowland Lancashire farm. Yet these farming communities have always expressed a sense of

LEFT: PASTORAL NORTH
A pale winter's sun edges towards a distant laithe-house on the Lancashire moors near Sabden. The laithe-house, a direct descendant of the longhouse, evolved from the farmer's need to keep his stock close to the farmhouse.

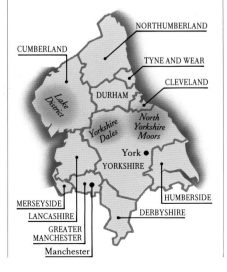

PENNINE STONE
Derbyshire, gritstone,
l brown sandstone,
...e the farms and barns of
the lower Pennines. The habit of
projecting the through or bonding
stones beyond the surface of
the wall was common in the
north of England.

affinity with each other, their mutual enemy being the weather. On this cold, wet edge of Europe, the elements have the capacity to ruin a man overnight: a late crop of hay spoiled by torrential rain; a herd of sheep suffocated under a snowdrift; the house cow drowned in a flood.

When in the eleventh and twelfth centuries the monastic landowners established their religious strongholds and introduced their sheep-breeding skills to the laity, the ram and ewe fertilized the ground and buttressed the local economy. The people lived by their flocks in single-unit dwellings with no division between the laithe, or barn, and what they called the firehouse, later the forehouse and finally the house. In the Pennines too, the preference for the communal aisled hall persisted into the 1600s, 200 years after it had disappeared from the south.

Once rid of their feudal friars, the rural yeomen took over the craft of shepherding, converting fleeces and sheep's milk, used for cheesemaking, into hard currency. Their produce was carried away by the teams of packhorses and their 'jaggers', drivers who took their payloads of lead, lime and wool to the west, returning with goods like

Cheshire salt. Many packhorse bridges, their parapets set low so as not to snag the panniers, still cross the wild moorland streams.

Since farming was such an unpredictable business, the sixteenth- and seventeenth-century farmer often earned additional income by working the mineral mines. The tortuous earth movements which bullied the Pennine hills into place also squeezed valuable deposits of lead, zinc and barium into the subsurface, and lead mining, which peaked around 1800, resulted in the building of remote hamlets like Greenhow Hill in the Dales. Invariably, these humble habitations included accommodation for the miner's ox or horse and a cow or two. The farmer-miner gave these cramped and dangerous mine shafts wryly humorous names like Wanton Legs or Nell I'll Tickle Thee, although he entered them in the full knowledge that this working day might be his last. Above ground, millstones made from the Pennine gritstone provided a safer sideline. Nevertheless, the

LEFT: FIELD BARN
From November to May, cattle were over-wintered in the two-storey field barn and turned out on to the buttercupped sward in spring. This Derbyshire barn, built into a bank to enable the farmer to fork hay directly into the upper floor, is surrounded by the straight, stone walls of the Parliamentary Enclosures.

LEFT: HONEY-BROWN GRITSTONE
Taken fresh from the quarry, gritstone was easily cut into long sections ideal for forming door and window surrounds. However, as this Derbyshire farmhouse chimney shows, the stone was prone to blacken if exposed to atmospheric pollution.

debtors' records from those days show bailiffs repossessing such meagre items as 'one brass pot' or 'a chest and truckle bed'. Clearly the average farmer did not expect to make a fortune.

In the seventeenth century, the smallholders and graziers of Derbyshire, Lancashire, Yorkshire, Cumbria, Durham and Northumberland were the poorest in the land. Their low-growth economy and primitive, if sustainable, agricultural practices were kind to the countryside but hard on the farmer and his family. They held fast to traditional customs because they could not afford to do otherwise. Farmhouse food was still being eaten from the traditional trencher or wooden plate when the Midland farmwife had thrown hers on the fire and changed to pewter. And the northern preference for unleavened rye bread and oatcakes persisted for at least a century after their southern neighbours had adopted the habit of adding yeast to their ground wheat. These Nonconformist northerners, accustomed to battling with poverty, bad weather and poor land, were in no hurry to change and it is not surprising they should be characterized as being a stern, stoical and self-sufficient people.

The Great Rebuilding did not reach the north until about 1640, a hundred years later than the south. The northerner's isolation was partly responsible for the delay but economic factors also played their part—the rebuilding corresponds with the time when woollen cloth had become England's biggest export. As in other parts of England, social hierarchy complicates accurate dating: the larger hall houses and yeomen's farms were built earlier; tenanted farms and large cottages caught up later; while the humblest smallholders often waited until the early nineteenth century to modernize their homes.

Having decided to incorporate a little privacy and comfort into their old residences, dividing and subdividing rooms into buttery, kitchen, house, chamber and parlour, the farmers used their mutton money to meet the costs of such improvements. Not for nothing does the black head of a curly-horned Swaledale ram serve as the symbol of the Dales National Park. The base materials for the building boom ranged from the broken boulders of the high Pennines to lowland chalks and clays. West of the Pennines, timber, clay, and later cobble and brick, were used to construct the single-storey commoners'

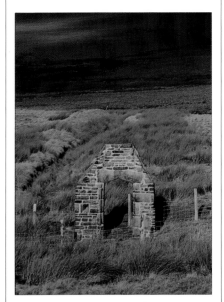

ABOVE: WINDSWEPT MOORLAND
The carved arched doorway and dressed stone door jamb are all that remain of this farmhouse on the Lancashire moors near Nelson. They stand as a monument to the tough way of life led by the moorland farmer.

RIGHT: SPRING FARM
The name of the farm often offers clues to its past. This neat, Lancashire holding was sited near to a dependable water supply.

ABOVE: BLUEBUTTS FARM
The gritstone doorframe, stout wooden door and well-worn step on this Lancashire farm emphasize the functional dignity of the northern farmhouse and its outbuildings.

NVNC MEA
MOX HVIVS
SED POSTEA
NESCIO CVIVS

NEMO SIBI NATVS

smallholdings of the Lancashire plains; to the east, generously proportioned farms, brick-built with Dutch pantiles and Norwegian softwood shipped up the river valleys of the Humber and Ouse, graced the rich, arable vales.

However, it was the local stone, especially the gritstone, limestone, sandstone and black, Cumbrian rock, which made the most memorable impact on the northern landscape. Pennine grits, strong enough to form millstones which the masons swore were as good as any French import, gave a sombre look to the farmyard; pale-grey sandstone brightened the Yorkshire Dales; blue-grey slate rock, tinged with green lichens and mosses, patterned the Cumbrian heartland; red sandstone characterized the farms around Cockermouth; pink granite was formed into farms near Eskdale; while the gritstone near Slaidburn in the Forest of Bowland came out a battleship grey.

Although the farmer might import Irish timber for his ceilings and panellings and send to the blacksmith for his iron casement windows, he took his house stone from the local quarry. Quarries, like vineyards, varied in quality: Derbyshire's Darley Dale or Bramley

Fall near Leeds were said to yield the classic gritstones; mountain limestone drawn from a quarry like Roche Abbey was regarded by Sir Christopher Wren as one of the best stones in England, second only to Portland stone. Where the village quarry cut across these noble bedrocks, the stonework of the modest farmhouse shared its good looks with some of England's finest buildings.

Much of the stonework has been disfigured by atmospheric pollution. Dolomite limestone sparkles with light when carried fresh and wet from the quarry, while gritstone starts out a light, honey brown. Both were blackened by their 200 years' exposure to the sulphurous air breathed out by the industrial cities that ringed the Peaks. Most susceptible of all was the gritstone which trails down the Pennines from North Yorkshire to form Dark Peak, a rocky horseshoe to the north, east and west of the limestone dome known as White Peak.

Although there was always the suspicion that what was new might prove to be no more than a passing fancy and change for change's sake, the northern farmers borrowed ideas from the south, altering

RIGHT: Beatrix Farm
An unassuming and unspoilt farmhouse sits on the hillside near Dunsop Bridge in the Forest of Bowland. The projecting line of through stones beneath the eaves would once have supported a length of wooden guttering.

RIGHT: Winter Weather
Cushioned in a late fall of snow, the barns and outbuildings of this low-headed Yorkshire Dales farm cluster around the farmyard. In such conditions, the farmer needs his stock and their feed close by.

them to suit their particular needs. Their conservatism had its rewards. When nineteenth-century domestic building began to be based more on pattern books than on traditional designs, architects like Charles Voysey and Edwin Lutyens journeyed north and borrowed details from the northern vernacular to decorate the southern suburban homes. There was, and still is, much to be learned from the local buildings of the north.

One of the traditional Pennine farms is the laithe-house, a later version of the longhouse. With the laithe-house, farm, barn and byre were built as separate units under the same sandstone roof. The gritstone was soft enough to cut into sections and long rectangles of the stone were used to frame doors and windows, rather than following the customary habit which had been to form the door jambs and window edges from the wall masonry. If the back and side walls, hidden from view, were roughly formed from inferior gritstone, a solid show was always made of the façade with its chequer-board effect of blackened ashlar against cream-coloured

RIGHT: CLUSTERED BUILDINGS
A mixed economy of cattle and sheep, pigs and poultry led to a proliferation of sheds, sties, barns and stables in the wooded vale of Farndale in North Yorkshire.

RIGHT: FARNDALE
The farmhouses of north-east Yorkshire are in striking contrast to their counterparts higher up in the Dales. Spread out among the green pastures of these lower dales, the rose-coloured roofs of these longhouse-style farms mark time in the greenery of the valley.

LEFT: SMELTER FARM
This farm and its neighbours in Bishopdale valley are the best examples of the seventeenth-century farmhouses in the Yorkshire Dales built by yeoman farmers, who managed to buy out the tenancies on their holdings in the early 1600s. The name of the farm suggests strong connections with the local mineral trade.

LEFT: DATESTONES
The Great Rebuilding reached the north about a century after the south. The year, set beneath the stone mullions of a farmhouse window near Arncliffe, confirms its arrival in the Yorkshire Dales. The rebuilding of these fine farms reached a peak towards the end of the seventeenth century.

pointing. Low-pitched roofs and gables that finished in neat kneeler stones all contributed to the Derby farmhouse's distinctive, darksome looks.

Limestone, by contrast, gave a moon-lit sheen to the farmhouse walls. This fossilized accretion of sea shells runs up through central Derbyshire into North Yorkshire, its geological boundaries with the gritstone showing through in farms, farm buildings and drystone walls. Although some walls are of monastic origin and date back to the twelfth and thirteenth centuries, the majority were built to divide up heath and grazing common during the late eighteenth- and early nineteenth-century Parliamentary Enclosures. Around Chelmorton, where the village street was onced lined with farms, the limestone walls are thickset, silvery and laid out in the neat, narrow rectangles of the Enclosures. And they are more prone to slump beneath their own weight than the darker gritstone walls with their complexities of jumpers, throughs, and plain-top or cock-and-hen copings.

The Enclosure walls which stream down the hillsides and network the valley bottoms of the Yorkshire Dales were imposed on a farmed landscape put in place by Scandinavian settlers moving into the area from Cumbria during the tenth century. The wide, wild beauty of this glacier-scoured landscape lies in the broad, flat-topped hills, scarred limestone pavements, dramatic scree slopes and the farms—pale-grey farmhouses, distant stone smallholdings and scattered field barns. The Dales' Nordic past is commemorated in old Norse names like Langstrothdale and Arkengarthdale, Apersett and Greensett—setts or saetrs were the Scandinavian's high, summer grazing pastures. The Norse word for valley was dale and words like beck, fell, crag and mere come from the same ancient roots.

The earliest surviving farmhouses are those like the fortified Nappa Hall in Wensleydale, which combined the attributes of a fort with a farm and led to the dry remark by the architectural historian, Nikolaus Pevsner, that 'these northern counties devoted their efforts more to security and solidity than to display.'

Before the eighteenth-century water-powered mills crushed the cottage weavers' trade, many a farmer worked his 'quishion loome' when he had seen to his animals and crops—upholstered chairs were

LEFT: FOREIGN IMPORTS
Pantiles carried in from the ports on the eastern seaboard brought a bright and more durable finish to the farm roofs which were originally thatched with ling.

ABOVE: RIDGE HOUSE FARM
Hipped roofs are almost unknown in North Yorkshire. An ashlar wall of sandstone, a neat parapet and a carefully carved kneeler stone give an unfussy finish to the simple gable of the farmhouse illustrated opposite.

RIGHT: BLEA TARN
A Lakeland farm with byre below took its running water from the fellside brook. The typical floor plan of the Cumbrian longhouse was of the living quarters or 'fire house' at the upper end, divided from the cowshed or 'down-house' by a cross-passage which ran from the front to the back of the house.

RIGHT: FRAMED IN STONE
An unglazed, wooden window is set in a frame of irregular coursed rubble on a Lakeland bank barn at Troutbeck. The two-storey bank barns were built into a slope with a ground-floor entrance for the stock at the front and an upper entrance to the fodder store at the back. A hatch between the floors allowed the farmer to feed his animals from above.

a luxury and there was a ready demand for something to soften the hardwood farmhouse seat. During the late seventeenth and early eighteenth centuries, the work of the West Yorkshire weaving farmers proved profitable. Living conditions gradually improved. The weaver might begin in a tiny one-roomed cottage, open to the roof and crowded out with loom, shearboard, chest and truckle. The truckle was a low, space-saving bed which slid beneath a work bench during the daytime and was a necessary piece of equipment for the farmers who wove a little cloth to supplement their income.

With good luck and a steady trade, the farmer-weaver could aspire to a two-storey farmhouse, three times the length of the original building, with a barn, shippon and pighouse added on. He might even afford a washing house, larder and brewery equipped with a malt kiln outside. Inside, new looms would be installed on the second floor where long rows of weavers' windows would light his work.

When the rush of rebuilding reached the Dales in the seventeenth and eighteenth centuries, farms and farmhouses continued to be built in a functional rather than fashionable way. Whereas in the Midlands and eastern lowlands farmers had doubled the depth of their farms, placing a second house before or behind the original in what was known as the double pile plan, the northern highlander preferred his traditional plan of a long rectangular building, up to three bays long yet still no more than one room deep.

Pastoral farming alone requires few outbuildings but these busy, mixed-economy farms needed a wide range of farm buildings. The farmer wanted somewhere clean to butcher his meat and somewhere cool to store it—several Dales farms still possess their beef loft, used to store pickled carcasses. He had to have a flag-stoned salting room, a dairy, a haywain, a place to winnow corn and store the straw and a covered place to keep his oxen and cart. By the end of the eighteenth century, the farmer could expect to have moved into a house with kitchen, milkhouse and buttery, two parlours, one at either end of the house, and two or three chambers, one or two to store corn, rye, salt flesh, hemp yarn and bread, and one, with two beds and a fireplace, to sleep in. Extra residents, like a maid or labourer, would be billeted with the stores in one of the chambers.

ABOVE: KENTMERE
A typical Cumbrian longhouse nestles with its neighbour in a Lakeland valley. Such remoteness meant that innovative farming ideas were slow to filter through, but it helped to preserve regional identity long after other areas had lost theirs.

BELOW: STEPPED GABLE
A staircase-like, crow-step gable and a purpose-built owl nesting box provide decorative details to this imposing Cumbrian barn.

RIGHT: PELE TOWER
When this pele tower was built at Kentmere Hall, Cumbria, in the troubled fourteenth century, the local farming population could retreat to its first and second floors until danger had passed. Scottish raiding parties were unlikely to break through the walls, sometimes up to five feet thick.

LEFT: OVERLOOKING ULLSWATER
Glencoyne Farm was built in 1629 for one of the new breed of independent Cumbrian farmers, known as Statesmen.

ABOVE: SINGULAR BEAUTY
William Wordsworth found the cylindrical Cumbrian chimney singularly beautiful. It appears in those areas where the underlying stone was too hard to be cut for a rectangular chimney. Similar designs are found in Wales and the west of England.

Sometimes the old farmhouse was abandoned, its stonework re-cycled into a new farm and barn, centred around a stone-floored backyard and appropriately named New Field, Stonehouse Farm or New Laithe. In the early eighteenth century, a spinning gallery might be incorporated into the first floor with a long, stone-mullioned window to light the work of the spinners. Where the Georgian style slipped in, the Dutch vertical sash window was judged to be too deep for the traditional low-browed Dales farmhouse and the northerner adapted it to his own design with the Yorkshire sash, a horizontal sliding window more suited to his farmhouse.

The Dales roof was shallow-pitched to take the heavy flagstones, locally known as grey slates. These flags, quarried from sandstone and shelled down into thick slates with a chamfered bottom edge, were hooked over the roof battens with a wooden peg or a piece of bone. The wide-shouldered, double-storey porch, set over the farmhouse door, might be lit by an oriel window. Occasionally a curiously carved door head and date panel, especially common around Littondale, Ribblesdale and Wharfedale, was placed on the face of the building. Otherwise decoration was kept to a minimum.

'These humble dwellings remind the contemplative spectator of a production of Nature and may be said to have grown rather than to have been erected—to have risen by an instinct of their own, out of the native rock,' wrote William Wordsworth in 1835. His obser-vations, poetic and precise, apply equally well to the grey Dales farm or the Peak District laithe-house, but, as a native Cumbrian, he was referring to the farms of the Lake District.

On the agriculturally rich Cumbrian coast or up amongst the coal-mining areas to the north, sandstone walls and green Westmorland slate roofs predominated. The sandstone, soft and porous, was usually rendered or colourwashed in pinks and reds, while window surrounds, door jambs and corner stones were, and continue to be, framed in strident reds, blues, browns and greens. Wordsworth would have disapproved. Quoting Sir Joshua Reynolds on the subject of house colour, he recommended that one 'see what is the colour of the soil where the house is to stand, and let that be your choice'. For entirely practical reasons, the Cumbrian farmer firmly

ABOVE: FRAMED IN PAINT
While the walls of farm buildings were left in their raw stone state, the barn or stable door like this one at Glencoyne was, like the house, often framed in whitewash. The limewash not only protected the stone, but also helped the farmer to find his way at night.

ABOVE: UPLAND WALLS
*Lichens decorate the face of a
Lakeland drystone wall. Most
walls were laid in the nineteenth
century to enclose open grazing.
Others, built to mark out huge,
monastic holdings and more modest,
parish boundaries, were laid in
medieval times. A well-built wall
will last for a couple of centuries.*

ignored the poet's advice: the white limewash coat which dresses the walls of so many of the long, low-headed farmhouses, and often the stable doorway as well, not only kept out the driving rain but also guided the tired farmer home from the fells in the pitch-black, moonless nights.

A number of early timber-framed buildings, like the cruck-timbered barn at Field Head Farm, Hawkshead or the half-timbered Wall End at Great Langdale, still stand, as do some of the timber and clay cottages, or clay daubins, erected by villagers in a single day for couples about to be married. However, it was Cumbria's century of stone, from around 1650, which produced the distinctive rugged Lakeland farmhouse. An ashlar face is rare outside the slate-quarrying areas and the men who built here did not waste their lime mortar. Rough stone, laid to look like drystone walling, had the mortar set deep inside the joints; inner and outer stones overlapped the rubble wall core and were imperceptibly sloped to throw off rainwater; and throughs or tie stones were deliberately projected out from the barn and outbuildings. Building such walls from nature's random rubble was skilled work—a builder's level placed against these 300-year-old quoins shows they still run true.

Sometimes the roof of the byre is a foot or two higher than the house which, on the older farms, was occasionally finished with a staircase-like stepped parapet. Primitive label moulds made from a line of slate set in the walls hang over the windows, while rudimentary porch hoods, known as pentices, shelter barn and byre doors. A wide porch, whitewashed inside and out, protected the heavy wooden door, secured against unwelcome visitors by a drawbar on the inside. A spinning gallery, open to the elements, was often added to the north wall and provided a place for fleeces to be hung to dry.

'These dwellings,' observed Wordsworth, 'mostly built of rough, unhewn stone, are roofed with slates, which were rudely taken from the quarry before the present art of splitting them was understood, and are therefore rough and uneven in their surface, so that both the coverings and sides of the houses have furnished places of rest for the seeds of lichens, mosses, ferns and flowers.' Noting the 'singular

RIGHT: FOWLSTONE FARM
*Lake District farmhouses like this
one near Lupton often show
decorative features which a
Dalesman would find unnecessarily
fussy. Because of its use of local slate
and stone, the farmhouse, with its
mix of mullion and sash windows
and tall porch with datestone and
finial, manages to look in keeping
with its surroundings.*

beauty' of the tubby Cumbrian chimney he wrote: 'There is a pleasing harmony between the tall chimney of this circular form and the living column of smoke, ascending from it through the still air.'

Once it became preferable to vent the hearth smoke from the house rather than allow it to find its own way out through a hooded opening in the roof, the untutored builder had to solve the problem of how best to do it. In parts of Cornwall, West Wales and Cumbria, where the underlying stone was too hard to shape into the conventional rectangular chimney, masons who had never seen each other's work developed the same distinctive design, forming the stack with rounded, 'bread-oven' sides, capped with a pair of slates. The hearth, hooded with a great lath and plaster canopy which welled up through the floor of the chamber above, passed out of the gable wall into the chimney stack, corbelled out on the gable end.

Nowhere else in England were so many farmhouses built within a single period and to such a similar design. This was partly due to the Statesmen, a group of farmers who in Elizabethan times had acquired certain common rights and permission to bequeath land by will. When the fashion to rebuild reached the Lakes, their wool wealth, settled status and right to take stone led them to build big, beautiful homes like Townend in Troutbeck and Glencoyne in Patterdale.

These Cumbrian farms, rich in architectural expression, are in sharp contrast to the unadorned farms of the border counties. The small hamlets and isolated farmsteads, which settled themselves close to some convenient stream in the foothills of the Cheviots, lived under constant threat of border raids right up until the eighteenth century. One solution was to build a pele, a two- or three-storey tower with storage space on the ground floor and living quarters above. Another defensible farm was the bastle where the family again lived on the first floor, quartering the stock on the ground floor—it was better to lose your cattle and live to see another day than perish with the cows.

The Northumbrian custom of sharing living space with the animals did not die out easily and, as late as the 1850s, the house cow or pig could still expect to be stalled in the labourer's single-storey cottage. Elsewhere in the north of England, especially around Durham,

ABOVE: PETTY HALL
A pentice of Lake District slate forms an eyebrow over a former stable door, topped with a datestone and the owner's initials. The corn barn and stable were often given greater architectural adornment than the cowhouse or cartshed. Both have been made redundant by twentieth-century farming methods and the maintenance of these obsolete buildings is a burden on the farmer's ingenuity as well as his purse.

RIGHT: LIMESTONE WALLS
The farmhouse at Petty Hall, built over a century earlier than the stable and barn to which it is attached, was constructed of limestone and given a roof of Cumbrian slate. The initials carved into the lintel were probably those of the farmer and his wife.

farmhouses, designed like the bastle house for first-floor living, continued to be built long after the danger of border attacks had passed. Why this tradition should have carried on well into the nineteenth century is something of a mystery. One suggestion is that heat from the animals gathered below rose up to warm the family above; another, that the tradition for first-floor living was so entrenched, nobody could think of a good reason to abandon it. Like the pele tower and bastle house, most, if not all, such buildings have been either absorbed into a later farmhouse or turned into farm buildings. However, there is often some remaining sign of their former status: a hatch let into the first floor leading directly to the

animal quarters below; a flight of steps leading up the outside wall to what once served as the farmer's front door; or an absence of ground-floor windows.

As with the farmhouses of eastern England in the following chapter, the ancestry of most Northern farmhouses lies in the traditional hall house and longhouse. The fact that each area developed such radically different designs is a testimony to regional distinctiveness and one which mocks the bland and unadventurous look of their twentieth-century counterparts.

LEFT: NORTHUMBRIA
No farm could afford to be sited far from water and many, like Shillmoor in Upper Coquet Dale, took advantage of a passing moorland stream. On the Northumberland moors, many farms also possessed a small cottage or shieling on the high pastures which was used during the summer months.

LEFT: HILLSIDE FORT
The crenellations and mock battlements of Lemmington Branch near Alnwick screen the farmhouse and barns from public view. Built long after the threat of attack from the Scottish borders had passsed, the farm is a reminder of the days when many of Northumbria's remote farms needed to be fortified.

CHAPTER SIX

EASTERN ENGLAND

Go where I will, thy landscape forms a part
Of heaven: e'en these Fens, where wood nor grove
Are seen, their very nakedness I love.
JOHN CLARE

F ARMERS, ON THE WHOLE, do not become famous men. The farmer is the man who feeds us all and, tied to his place of work, he has little time for anything else. Nevertheless, a few agriculturalists have found a place in the history books: Charles Townshend, Jethro Tull, William Cobbett, Thomas Tusser, William Marshall, Thomas Coke and Arthur Young among them. With the exception of Cobbett and Tull, they share the distinction of having had the East Anglian soil beneath their fingernails—this rounded rump of England has long been renowned for its fertility.

Eastern England could be said to begin at the end of the London Underground in Essex and end at the beginning of Humberside. A high-speed train journeying from London to Lincoln sprints briefly through housing estates before plunging into a kaleidoscope of blue-greens and bottle-greens, Prussian blues and muddy browns, citrine yellows and mellow golds merging into a background of deep, dark oak woods and willow-fringed rivers, sparkling blue broads and wide, ploughed fields, flowering oilseed rape and sheets of ripening corn. This eastern palette is a blur of natural colour and it has inspired artists from John Constable to the Norwich School of painters who celebrated the sharp clear light of East Anglia.

There are four distinct regions within the counties of Essex, Suffolk, Norfolk, Cambridgeshire and Lincolnshire: the lush valleys, meandering streams and meadowland of the south and east; the

LEFT: FENLAND FARMSCAPE
The eastern counties are more productive than any other area of England. The fertile soil, now mostly devoted to large-scale arable farming, has fattened every kind of farmyard animal, grown every crop in the seed catalogue and produced some fine farmhouses. Purton Green Farm at Stansfield in Suffolk, restored by the Landmark Trust in 1969, is one of the earliest surviving thirteenth-century aisled farmhouses.

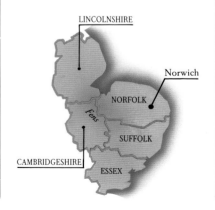

chalky heathlands and prairie fields of the central and north-eastern areas; the wide, austere fens of the west; and the chalk wolds of Lincolnshire banked up against the ridge of limestone hills which are the most northerly extension of the great limestone belt.

'So moping flat and low our valleys lie,/ So dull and muggy is our winter sky,' wrote John Clare, the Fenland farm labourer turned poet. Much of East Anglia is flat, but it is not featureless. The highest point is some 400 feet above sea level and a considerable acreage of the land lies, protected by flood walls, below sea level and yet the landscape possesses its own distinctive details—a weatherboarded mill in Essex, a timber-framed manor in Suffolk, a flint-walled Norfolk church, a thatched farm in Cambridgeshire, a pantiled roof in Lincolnshire. Each has direct links with a rich agricultural past, for this is a land founded on the fortunes of farmers.

The casual impression of East Anglia as a giant wheatfield beholden to the British baking industry is a false one. Ever since the arrival of the Angles who gave their name to the fenland and forest of the North Folk and South Folk, the farmers have grown every crop in the seed catalogue and raised every animal in the farming manual from shire horses to salt-fed lambs. Frequently in the vanguard of agricultural innovation, the East Anglian farmer tilled a fertile soil, formed by a thick cream of boulder clay spread over well-drained chalk during the last Ice Age. The terrain was smooth, the climate kind and, with major markets and convenient ports close to hand, the farmer rode out intermittent recessions and capitalized during times of plenty. The Essex farmers, like those in Hertfordshire, shipped produce to the London markets by sea and canal and brought back barges of street manure. Goose down, plucked from live geese, and larks snared on the Fens were exported from King's Lynn and Boston, harbours which carried almost as much trade as London in the thirteenth century. The bright, yellow dye taken from the purple or saffron crocus brought prosperity to the Essex town of Saffron Walden while the medieval wool trade, focused on East Anglia in the thirteenth and fourteenth centuries, produced a corresponding architectural boom in church and farmhouse building. Until competition from the Cotswolds overtook the local

ABOVE: DECEPTIVE APPEARANCE
Despite the alarming lean on the two-storey porch, the condition of this sixteenth-century farmhouse at Wormingford in Essex is not a cause for concern. Since it was easier to cut and carve oak while it was still green, most timber-framed houses were built in unseasoned oak. The timbers were allowed to season and settle in position.

LEFT: COLVILLE HALL
Essex possessed an abundance of English oak, but little good building stone. This fifteenth-century farmhouse at White Roding is one of the county's numerous timber-framed buildings. Close studding, infilled with handmade bricks laid horizontally and diagonally, give the farmhouse a distinctive look.

industries, the blankets and blue cloth of Bildeston and the jerseys of Kersey, both in Suffolk, were noted throughout the country.

New crops and new techniques were tried out in East Anglia before being adopted around the country. The old regime of putting to the pole-axe draught and dairy animals which could not be fed through the cold, dark months of winter was brought to an end by Charles Townshend, dubbed 'Turnip' Townshend when he grew the root crop on his Norfolk estate specifically as a winter feed. The early eighteenth-century agriculturalist also championed the benefits of crop rotation which became standard farming practice across the land and transformed agriculture.

The eighteenth-century Norfolk landscape, quartered by deep drainage ditches and teeming with windmills, bore a striking resemblance to the lowlands of Holland and emphasized the

LEFT: HIDDEN TIMBERS
Many of the timber-framed farms of Essex were clad in weatherboarding or, as on the sixteenth-century Houchins Farm at Feering, a weatherproof coat of plaster. The red tiles and half-hipped gable roof are common enough, but the jettying out of both first and second floors is unusual. Outside the old farm stand the staddle stones, once used to support the granary and keep rats and mice at bay.

140

influence that Europe's Low Countries have had on East Anglia. Today, apart from the flowering bulbfields of Lincolnshire, the one lasting reminder of those ties is the farmhouse.

The centuries-old trade with the Netherlands and Flanders made a significant impression on the farmers' homes. As Suffolk sheep and Norfolk pigs went out, timber, brick and new architectural ideas came in. The chalklands and heathlands of those two counties yielded only flint as a building stone and the imports were gratefully received and rapidly adopted. Flint was fine for prehistoric people— flint implements from the Grimes Graves mines in Norfolk were traded right across the British Isles—but used alone it was an inadequate building stone. Whether knapped into roughly regular pieces or used uncut as random rubble, it was a troublesome material to form into quoins and corners for doors and windows. The Roman builder had used clay tiles to bond the flint; his sixteenth-century successor used brick.

Good clay for brickmaking was plentiful and the East Anglians, learning their technique from the Continent, became the first of the English regions to establish their own brickyards. (Long Bridge at Coggeshall in Essex is said to be the oldest brick bridge in England, built after the Cistercian monks at Coggeshall Abbey brought back the art of brickmaking from their European monasteries.) Initially, the owners of larger, manorial farms imported their bricks, using them to complement existing materials by adding a brick-built gable to a timber-framed farmhouse or building tall, elaborate brick chimneys with hexagonal, circular or spiral stacks. The idea of employing different coloured bricks to form decorative patterns on farmhouse walls reached England from northern France in the late fifteenth century and the diamond pattern in particular became so popular that, even in flint walls, the diaper design was often picked out in brick.

By the seventeenth century, local brickmaking was in full swing. Dug from the building site in winter, the brick clay was left to season until spring when it was wetted, trodden out to remove any foreign matter and pressed into wooden moulds ready for firing. By the end of the seventeenth century, horse-powered pugmills had mechanized

ABOVE: OPPORTUNIST BUILDER
A farm building near Parham in Suffolk demonstrates a make-do-and-mend approach to repairs. Dressed stone has been recycled and used on the original brick and flint building, possibly to block off a redundant cartshed door.

ABOVE: PARGETING
Wet plaster provided a base for relief or incised decorative work, known as pargeting. Essex and Suffolk in particular possess some fine examples of the craft. This panel, on an old farmhouse near Walpole in Suffolk, is dated 1708.

the laborious process of treading the clay, but the brick-kilns were still being fed with parish clays whose colours varied from region to region. In Cambridgeshire and west Norfolk, the clay burnt out to a pale yellow which they called white; closer to the coast, the clay baked a rich, ruddy brown.

One of the more spectacular Flemish influences was the Dutch gable and the crow-stepped gable, a brick-built design which spread inland to replace the conventional gable on many seventeenth-

LEFT: OLD CHAPEL
Built first as a farmhouse in 1607, the secular gave way to the religious forty years later when a group of Nonconformists turned it into their meeting house at Walpole, Suffolk.

LEFT: MOAT FARM
Late timber-framing and early brickwork were brought together to form this sixteenth-century farmhouse near Parham, Suffolk. The blocked-off windows may have been an attempt by some eighteenth-century occupant to reduce his liability for the window tax, introduced in 1696 and finally repealed in 1851.

century farms. The farmhouse roof was thatched and it was suggested that these towering gables pinched the thatch between them, holding it in place when the unseasonal, but all too regular, east wind blew. However, these gables, often with a chimney running up through their centre, look disproportionately tall, especially where a thick thatch has been replaced by a thin, clay tile roof. An alternative explanation is that the Dutch gables were more fashionable than functional and, the taller the better, were added to farmhouses and barns to impress the neighbours. On more modest farms, straight gables were built with triangles of brickwork 'tumbling-in', or laid horizontally at right angles to the gable. Another Dutch import, it provided a good, straight verge for the roofer.

RIGHT: SUFFOLK PINK
Bull's blood, chalk, soot and charcoal were traditional pigments used to colour the farmhouse limewash. A dark Suffolk pink has been used on Nether Hall Farm, a sixteenth-century, half-timbered building at Cavendish, Suffolk.

RIGHT: DUTCH GABLES
Chequered brickwork and rounded Dutch gables at Westerfield Hall, Suffolk, testify to the strong Flemish influence in East Anglia. This was the first English region to import bricks from the Netherlands and to set up its own brickyards. Farmhouses like this one, dated 1683, would have been unknown further west at that time.

The prestigious exterior of this
Norfolk farmhouse, dated 1699, is a
reflection of the prosperity of the
region in the seventeenth century.
The curiously steep pitch of the
pantile roof suggests an earlier
thatched roof of straw or
Norfolk reed.

Another elevated feature of the eastern farmscape was the thatched rick of hay or straw. It was still a feature of the landscape ten years after the last world war, although the Dutch barn, its high-arched tin roof echoing the shape of the convex Flemish gable, had been filtering across the region in the early nineteenth century. It in turn had replaced the traditional East Anglian barn, long and large enough to store and thresh the grain crop in the winter months. Most were large; some were enormous. The fifteenth-century Hales barn at Hales Hall in Norfolk is 180 feet long, took 700,000 bricks to build and not only stored the corn crop, but also stabled a dozen horses and housed several of the owner's employees.

Long-handled fire-hooks, used to tear smouldering thatch from burning houses or ricks, still hang on walls of local barns and churches. Despite the fire risk—Cambridge city banned thatch for this very reason in 1619—thatch remains a ubiquitous roofing material in Norfolk and Suffolk. There are six times as many thatched churches in these two counties as there are in the whole of England, and Suffolk in the 1960s still boasted more thatched roofs than any other county. The reason for such a wealth of thatch was that the best roofs in Britain were cut from Fenland reeds or Norfolk spear as it was called. These roofs, laid at a steep fifty-degree pitch, needed no rainwater guttering and were expected to outlast a wheaten thatch by thirty or forty years. Nevertheless, they still needed rethatching every sixty to eighty years and a significant number of farmers eventually settled for a new roof of tiles.

The small, plain clay tile, at first handmade, appeared in the south of the region while yet another Dutch-inspired material, the pantile, was adopted in coastal areas from Essex right round to Lincolnshire and beyond. Imported from Holland in the seventeenth century until local tileworks became established in the eighteenth century, the pantiles first appeared on farm buildings and cottages. As the advantages of a roof which was lightweight, long-lasting and aesthetically pleasing became appreciated, the pantile spread to the roofs of the larger farmhouses. Like bricks, the colour varied depending on the clay. Cambridgeshire produced a greyish yellow tile, while a brighter, red tile appeared in the north. In Norfolk,

tilemakers developed the habit of giving the pantile a black glaze and many farmhouse roofs in the Boston area took these dark tiles, torched with clay on their undersides to keep the snow from slipping in beneath them. As for the walls of these eastern farmhouses, the brick and flint of the central areas was sandwiched between timber and plaster in the south and limestone and brickwork in the north.

Although much of the woodland in the central region had been cleared by the sixteenth century, the oak woods of the south-east had fared far better and far longer. The business of building in oak was as strong here as it was in Kent and the West Midlands and the box-framed timbers on older farmhouses were built with the oak beams exposed and the panels filled with wattle and daub. Upwards of 300 small trees would be needed for a fine Suffolk farmhouse and as the cost of oak rose (it increased by over fifty per cent between the early sixteenth and late seventeenth centuries) the farmer looked at ways to economize. Where the frame itself was not built for show, the carpenter could reduce his timber needs by up to two-thirds and, from the sixteenth century, the half-timbered farms of Essex and Suffolk disappeared beneath a layer of plaster or weatherboard.

Weatherboarding involved sheathing the oak frame in oak or elm boards and later in lightweight deal. The practice was virtually confined to the south-eastern regions, although early East Anglian settlers took the technique with them to North America and gave the distinctive, clapboard look to the farms and houses of New England. Whereas a typical sixteenth-century farmhouse tends to have 'a wealth of exposed timbers' beneath a thatched roof with its characteristic sharp-pointed gables, its late seventeenth-century counterpart is more likely to have weatherboarded walls under a mansard roof of small clay tiles. The mansard roof, with two pitches either side of the ridge, the lower set steeper than the upper, was a common feature of the small Essex farmhouse, providing useful extra storage space in the loft.

Additional space in the Suffolk farmhouse was made by jettying out the first and occasionally the second floors. The habit of adding wings to the original hall gives them a comfortable, eiderdown look with their projecting gables, small tiles and tall brick chimneys.

ABOVE: PANTILES AND FLINT
The combination of brick, flint and old, red pantiles is typical of the eastern counties. The flint in the foreground, taken from the fields, has been laid uncoursed; the egg-shaped flint in the background, taken from the sea-shore or river bed, has been neatly coursed.

LEFT: NORFOLK VALLEY
Although little of the land in East Anglia rises more than three hundred feet above sea level, the countryside has its secret share of tranquil lanes and quiet farms like this one near Hunworth in Norfolk.

ABOVE: FACTORY BRICKWORK
When this farm building was put up in the nineteenth century, bricks were no longer being made by hand. The new bricks were cheaper, more uniform and of a predictable quality, but they lacked the character of a local brick, fired in the farmyard. Here at Fulmodestone, Norfolk, a wooden dovecot hangs on the brickwork.

ABOVE: CROW-STEPPED GABLE
Most farms in south-west Norfolk were built of brick and flint in the late seventeenth and early eighteenth centuries. But this farm building with its crow-stepped gables, blocked-off windows with brick pediments and ornamental chimney, was built at the beginning of the seventeenth century.

What the farmer lost on exposed timber beams, he made up for with colour washes painted on the plaster. From the familiar Suffolk pink, made by mixing animal blood or sloe juice into the plaster, through to apricot and orpiment, a bright lemon-yellow formerly made from a potentially lethal mixture of sulphur and arsenic, these washes added a welcome dash of colour to the buildings. In Cambridgeshire, plaster made from the local marl rather than lime gave the farmhouse a white and rather plain finish which might account for the practice of pargeting, when designs were formed with a nail or a sharp stick in the wet plaster. Once the plasterer had mastered simple incised decorations—zigzags, herringbones and floral borders—he was encouraged to attempt more fashionable relief work, pre-forming his designs in a mould or, if he had steady fingers and a good eye, by hand in the wet plaster. These designs, sometimes incorporating a date, were concentrated in Cambridgeshire, Essex and Suffolk and were doubtless intended to suggest to the passer-by that here was a yeoman farmer of some substance.

A plaster finish also concealed one other highly localized walling material, clay lump. Cut straw, small stones, horsehair and water were mixed in with clay, pressed into block-shaped moulds, allowed to dry in the sun and then laid like blockwork over a damp-proof plinth. Clay lump needed a good protection against the elements and the cheapest solution was to give it a coat of tar. Tucked under a cosy roof of Norfolk reed thatch or clay tile and hidden behind its weatherproof overcoat, this earthy material lasted a long time: some of the clay lump buildings of Norfolk, Suffolk and south-east Cambridgeshire have survived for 300 years. Since the boulder clay for the building could be dug on site and repaired, like modern blockwork, without too much difficulty, clay lump might be used by the farmer for a wide range of outbuildings from piggeries to turkey pens and was still being used for farm cottages in this century.

The farmhouses of Lincolnshire, characterized by their pantiled roofs, a deep red in the south and a darker red in the north, were formed in brick or, where they crossed the limestone belt, of pale, ashlar stone. The seventeenth- and eighteenth-century Lincolnshire farmhouse, built with its back to the farmyard and its fine façade to

RIGHT: BRICK AND FLINT
Flint was the only available stone in some parts of Norfolk. Impossible to form into corner stones or surrounds, it was invariably used with stone or brick. Here the brickwork decorates a blocked-off window.

LEFT: OLD MANOR FARM
*From the seventeenth century
onwards, and despite abundant
supplies of Norfolk reed, thatch was
gradually superseded by pantiles.
Inland, thatch persisted for far
longer. The ornamented crow-
stepped gables on this farmhouse at
Fen Drayton in Cambridgeshire
helped to hold the thatch in place.*

the road, reflects the richness of the soil and the diligence of its owner. The village farmer was no longer content with a local design fashioned in local materials, but expected to show his neighbours a symmetrical front elevation with a central doorway flanked by two windows on either side and five windows above. He ceased to care for cold earth floors and whitewashed walls and could afford to walk on brick or boards and decorate his walls with flock wall-papers instead. The vernacular tradition was coming to an end.

What became known as the Lincolnshire limestones, most of which were actually quarried in neighbouring Northamptonshire and the former county of Rutland, were exploited by the monasteries in the Middle Ages and shipped south along the waterways to build East Anglia's castles, cathedrals and colleges. The stone which, like other limestones, hardens with age and exposure, was a valuable commodity and commanded good prices—the monks at Ramsey for example paid their Peterborough brethren 4,000 eels for the privilege of using their limestone. Where the stone was used locally, it gave an unmistakable Cotswold look to the farmhouses with their stone mullions and limestone slate roofs. But further north, above Lincoln, the quality of the stone deteriorated and brickwork replaced the rough, rubble stone around windows, doors and corners. To the east and in the southern Fens, the stone ran out altogether.

The typical Fenland cottage was a whitewashed, one-and-a-half storey building with roof dormers and shuttered windows, constructed of whatever lay to hand—brick and pantile, mud and thatch, brick and flint. It looked out across a level sweep of land criss-crossed by gaudy tulip fields, dark vegetable plots and deep drainage ditches, a land on loan from the sea. When, in the nineteenth century, the windmill-driven water pumps were being replaced by steam pumps an inscription was cast into the casing of one of the engines which predicted:

> These Fens have oft times been by water drown'd,
> Science a remedy in water found.
> The powers of steam she said shall be employ'd
> And the Destroyer by itself destroyed.

ABOVE: OPEN HALL
*Like many of the Wealden houses in
the south of England, Manor Farm
at Brington in Cambridgeshire is a
former hall house where the original,
central room was open to the
roof rafters.*

LEFT: COTSWOLD ECHO
Lincolnshire's dominant stone is limestone. With its small stone slates, undulating ridge, stone mullions and gabled dormer window, Rectory Farm at Castle Bytham echoes the limestone look of the Cotswold tradition.

LEFT: HOLLAND FEN
With few trees and fewer hedgerows, Holland Fen in Lincolnshire is purpose-made, agricultural land. Drained with dykes like this one during the nineteenth century, the fertile loam is reputed to be the richest land in England.

LEFT: HALF-HIPPED ROOF
A sheltering belt of trees was planted to give the stockyard animals summer shade and winter protection. The first floor door on this brick and flint barn would have been used to take in hay for storage under the half-hipped roof of clay tiles.

The Fens, however, will never be safe from the Destroyer. In 1947 and 1953, the North Sea breached the defences, drowning people and flooding 57,000 acres of farmland. Despite each new technological development which strives to protect the land from the sea, the Fens continue to lead a precarious existence.

THREATENED HERITAGE

The flint and brick Fenland cottage, the clay lump Norfolk farm and the half-timbered Suffolk manor are three examples of this eastern vernacular tradition. Like the Wealden hall, the Devon cob, the Dartmoor longhouse, the Cotswold manor, the Derbyshire laithe-house and the Northumbrian pele tower, each arose from local need, evolved for 200 or 300 years and, by the nineteenth century, had died away. Those which have survived stand in stark contrast to the standardized ways of today, when a modern house in High Wycombe has its mundane replicas in Harwich and Hexham.

Working farmhouses, rarely ostentatious and seldom pretentious, are to be found everywhere in the English landscape. From ten-roomed manor houses to two-roomed smallholdings, farmhouses are as natural a feature of the rural scene as the village church. A hundred years ago, no one would have seriously suggested studying, and possibly preserving, the humble farmhouse; now such a proposition has become a matter of urgency.

Some traditional farmhouses have been brutally modernized with details like fake leaded windows set in white plastic frames and imitation coach lamps on a stone frontage constructed like vertical crazy paving. Such restorations amount to acts of architectural vandalism. The sympathetically restored farmhouse will continue to fit naturally into the farmed landscape; the farmhouse which has been unkindly treated will look, like a motorway in a meadow, out of keeping and out of place.

The face of farming has changed and many old farmhouses will not survive the new era. We would do well to learn what we can about them before it is too late.

GLOSSARY

AISLED CONSTRUCTION: building method used on churches and large barns to carry a broad roof; posts, set on pillars or piers which separate the main building from the side walls, support roof trusses.

ASHLAR: stone cut in blocks and laid with fine jointing in squared and level courses.

BOX-FRAME: timber-frame construction based on box-like structure as opposed to cruck frame.

BASTLE: fortified farm housing animals on the ground floor and humans above.

BYRE: cow-shed.

CASEMENT: window, hinged at the side.

CAT-SLIDE ROOF: roof over a lean-to extension.

CLAPBOARD: weatherboards fixed horizontally to the face of a building.

COB: walling material composed of clay, straw and small stones.

CORBEL: projection of stone, brick or timber to carry weight of an upper floor, roof, etc.

CROSS-PASSAGE: corridor running from front to back of a building which separates domestic rooms from utility areas.

CRUCK: curved timber section, used in pairs to form arched house frame.

DAUB: mud or clay.

DRIP STONES, DRIP MOULDS: stone set above windows and doors as a rain guard.

GABLE: triangular end of a building.

DUTCH GABLE: gable with curved outline, occasionally crowned by a pediment.

FINIAL: uppermost feature, often ornamental, of a pinnacle, gable, roof, etc.

HALL HOUSE: medieval house with main living room open from floor to roof.

HIPPED ROOF: pitched roof over gable end.

HALF-HIPPED ROOF: half-pitched roof over gable end.

JETTY: overhanging upper floor on a timber-framed house.

KNEELER: finishing stone on a gable end which projects beyond wall line.

LAITHE-HOUSE: a version of the longhouse with living accommodation and animal quarters under one continuous roof, but reached by separate entrances.

LATHS: strips of wood used as a key for plaster.

LINTEL: horizontal timber or stone support over door or window openings.

LONGHOUSE: farmhouse and byre under one continuous roof, separated by a cross-passage which serves as entrance to both sides of the building.

MORTISE AND TENON: standard joint used in timber-frame building.

MULLION: stone or wooden bar which divides a window vertically.

NOGGING: brick infill on panels between timberframe work.

PARGETING: ornamental plasterwork on outside of building.

PELE-TOWER: building in northern areas, fortified against attack.

QUOINS: dressed stone corner of walls.

SASH WINDOW: sliding window frame on cord and pulleys.

SHINGLES: rectangular wooden tiles used as roof or wall covering.

SHIPPON: northern version of cowshed.

THROUGH STONE, JUMPER: bonding stones laid through masonry to provide stability

WATTLE: sticks interwoven between framework on half-timbered building to provide key for daub.